CLEAN

ARCHITECTURE

Comprehensive Beginners Guide to Learn and Understand Clean Architecture

⇒ CONNOR WALLACE ⇐

Table of Contents

Introduction

Designing a working software architecture is one thing; designing a clean architecture is another. To design working software architecture, you don't have to be an expert in programming. You don't need to know all there is about programming before creating architecture with impeccable functionality. However, the fact that your system runs smoothly does not mean the components are thoroughly integrated to avoid imminent problems that might lead to its crashing. The effort required to create a working architecture is not as much as the efforts required to create a clean architecture. Creating a clean architecture requires some level of specialty and competence. This, in software development, is a different ball game entirely.

This book extensively explains all the necessary skills needed to create clean architecture. The level of proficiency needed to build an efficient and effective clean architecture is very different from that required to create a working architecture. Not all working architecture is clean architecture, but all clean architectures work very well and run very smoothly than software designed just for the working benefits alone. The aspect of creating a clean architecture requires thoughts and skills, but unfortunately, many young programmers are not interested in this aspect. What many programmers focus on is creating a working architecture with a high level of productivity while little or no attention is paid to how clean the software is. Developing an impeccable software requires dedication, commitment, and discipline. It requires the desire for self-investment, the passion for the art, and the ambition to become an expert. Without these three keys, a programmer will only remain in the peripheral and will be sidelined as technology develops and progresses.

When a clean architecture is designed, something exceptional happens. Aside from the flawless and smooth improvement of the software, the programmer becomes aware that it doesn't take a huge bunk of documents or magical tracking ability to be able to develop brilliant software. Among the splendid benefits of a clean architecture is that it only requires a fraction of human resources and a bit of constant maintenance to keep it running. These benefits might sound a little unachievable or utopian, but it is not as difficult as it sounds.

The concentration of this book is to help interested programmers horn their ability and intelligence into creating a smooth and clean software. The book explained the steps entail in creating a clean architecture. By the end of the book, the programmer will realize how easy it is to create and design a brilliant software. It is as a result of this that the name of the book itself is called 'clean programming.'

The book provides a step by step explanation of what good software is, how it is developed, and things to take into consideration when developing your software. Each offers a detailed explanation of what programming entails and at the end of the explanations readers will be able to build strong software with a design and architecture that minimize effort and maximize productivity. You will also be able to design a system that will have solid productivity and a long, profitable lifetime warranty.

The book is divided into three sections: Designs, Architecture, and Details. Chapter one to six covers the first section, seven to thirteen covers the second section, while chapters fourteen and fifteen covers the last section

Chapter 1

What is Design and Architecture?

This chapter explains in detail the difference between design and architecture. It explains the features of good software and reveals the most important among these features. The outline to cover in the chapter include:

- What is design?

- What is architecture?

- The two major qualities of software programming

To start with, design and architecture the same thing. No difference exists between these two terms. When people try to explain the difference between the two, what they usually draw reference to is, the word architecture is more technical and used to refer to a high level of designs devoid of the little details usually seen in what is often refer to as designs. However, as convincing as this sounds, the truth remains that there is no work of architecture without designs. Let's take, for instance, the architectural work of our house. When presented with the layout of the house, what we usually see on the big picture are smaller details like the design of our living room, kitchen space dining space, room space, and many more. All these designs are what make up the architecture of our home. Just like these little details that both the intern and external structure of our home, the same way every software architecture is made up of the little details often referred to as design.

The low-level details and explanation, plus the high-level structures and appearance, are all part of what comes together to form the complete whole. They are what are fixed together to form the continuous fabric that defines the shape of the system often refer to as software.

Architecture and designs are interwoven; we can't have one without the other. Also, there is no clear cut line separating the one from the other. Designs form architecture and architecture design.

Major Qualities of Software Programming

There are two major qualities of every clean architecture. These qualities include the structure of the software and the behavior of the software. Whether or not a system has these two qualities is in the hand of the Software developers. Developers know more about these two concepts. They know that what determines good software is how well it portrays these key qualities. Unfortunately, most developers usually focus on one value and, in fact, many won't not even pay attention to any of these two qualities. Before going into the process involved in creating a clean software architecture, we will first consider the importance of these two qualities to the software system.

Behavior

This is the first major quality of a software program. The behavior of the system encompasses the performance action of the software. It determines how the system will work and the various functions the system will be able to perform. In fact, this value is one of the major things stakeholders look out for when hiring a software programmer. Programmers are often employed just to help control the ability of the system to make and save money. To do this, the programmers focus more on the functional requirements of the system and include codes that will help achieve the stakeholders' request. When the machine fails to perform as expected, the programmer uses his or her debugger to fix whatever may be the cause for the failed performance or underperformance.

As a result of the popularity of this value, most programmers usually this is where it en. They believe that once you can control how your program behaves and determine the function it performs, you have created a clean software. This is not the case. Developing clean software requires much more than just the behavior; the structure of the program plays a significant role.

Structure

The structure of the system encompasses everything that makes up the software itself. The structure is the software. To explain, the word software will be split into its two components: soft and ware. The second word, "ware," means commodity, product, or stocks. But the first word is the concentration of the structure of the system.

It means something flexible, easy, smooth, and delicate. Soft also means malleable and effortless. This implies that the name software was chosen for systems and programs because it was intended to be an easy task. Software means a product or program that can be easily changed or altered. It is designed to be malleable and not difficult. If systems were created to be a very difficult task, it will have been called hardware and not software.

Therefore, for software to fulfill its true purpose, it must be soft and not difficult to work on. When a stakeholder wants to change the feature of his or her software, this should be a very flexible task. Any difficulties that are be encountered while carrying out the task should be limited to the scope of the change and not the structure of the change. The shape of the change is expected to be made easy and flexible.

It is the difference between scope and shape that determines how clean and comfortable software is. This is also the reason for the increase in the human resources needed to manage software. It is the reason why the cost of changing any components part of the software keeps growing. The cost of the first year of development is often cheaper than the second and the second will be cheaper than the third. The cost continues to increase as development increases.

From the perspective of the stakeholder requesting some change in the software, what he or she is requesting is as simple as providing a stream of changes to a roughly similar scope. But from the developer's viewpoint, the task requested is like a stream of jigsaw puzzle pieces that they must fit into a puzzle of ever-increasing complexity. Every new request is always harder to accomplish than the previous one because the shape of the system does not match the shape of the request. The more an architectural work is designed in a particular shape, the more difficult it will be to fix new structure into the shape of that architecture.

The Greater the Value

Now that we have explained the two major qualities to concentrate on when designing software, which between these two values should the developer concentrate on? Function or architecture? Is it much more important for the software to be up to the task or for the features in the software to be easy to change? Which is better? The behavior of structure?

Let's assume this question is directed to the stakeholder; he or she will choose function or behavior over structure or architecture because the behavioral quality is where the profit lies. However, when this question is directed to the developer, the answer will be on the structure over the function. These differences in choice contributed to the problems of most software development today.

Take, for instance, the software designed for a stakeholder focused on function over the structure. This means that when the program requirements are altered, the system will stop working and becomes useless. But let's assume the system focus more on structure than function; it functions that when the need for change arises, and the program is altered, it will still perform effortlessly and keeps running smoothly. As the requirements for the program changes, the software can be easily changed to match the requirements. Such software will continually be useful.

However, some systems are quite impossible to alter. They are structured in such a way that there is a limit to the number of times it can be changed. When the time limit runs out, the software becomes practically impossible to change. In fact, the cost of changing them usually exceeds the benefits of changing them. As the requirements of the software change, it will reach a point whereby it will be very difficult to change them. Most systems are configured in such ways.

While the business manager often requests for functionality over flexibility when the need for change occurs, and he or she calls the developer to change the system. If the value for the change is too high, the business manager gets furious and will blame the developer for creating a system that is too difficult to alter. The difference in choice of the developer and the stakeholder is captured in the Eisenhower's matrix.

Eisenhower's Matrix Of Importance Versus Urgency

In the matrix, Eisenhower presents two kinds of problems. The urgent problem and the important problem. The urgent is not important, and the important is not urgent.

This adage is packed with the reality we often face as software developers and even the reality of life itself. In programming, the things that are often very important are rarely urgent, while those that are urgent are usually not very important. In the two values of software, one is urgent, while the other is important. The first value, which is the behavior is urgent but not very important, while the second value, the structure is important but not always urgent.

We can also add that there is something that is both urgent and important at the same time. Others might not be urgent and also not be important. Therefore, we can arrange this magic into four categories

- Urgent and important
- Not urgent and important
- Not important and Urgent
- Not urgent and not important

In fixing the values of the software according to the above-highlighted categories, we can say that the first value (behavior) fits into the first and third positions, while the second value (structure) fits into the first and second categories.

Business managers often make the mistake of elevating the third position to the first position. They fail to separate features that are important from those that are not.

The stakeholders make choices that pay him or her at present without a glimpse into the feature. The developer considers both the future and the present. The developer knows more about the software and should handle the determining process. This will help avoid the dilemma often encountered when business managers make the decisions.

The last point to explain in this section is the software developer.

Who is a software developer? Two major categories make up the software developers team:

- The software developer
- The software architecture

The Software Developer

The software developers are the people skilled in the art of evaluating the importance of a software system. They know the best software for a company and usually handle the efficiency and effectiveness of a company's software. They determine the requirements for the company's software program and handle tasks related to changing these requirements into better ones.

The Software Architect

Subsumed in the software developers team is the software architect group. This group is concerned with the structure of the software. Their job is to determine the structure of the system and how this structure will be made flexible enough to allow the features and functions of the software to be easily operated on. The focus on making the software components flexible enough to allow changes when need be. They also control these changes and ensure it doesn't cause any harm to the software.

In other to create a clean architecture, the structure should come before function. If this is reversed, the system might too difficult to change or too expensive to maintain.

Summary

In this chapter, we have extensively covered what software architecture is, the qualities, and the function of the two departments subsumed within the software developers team. The next chapter will focus on getting started in clean architecture.

Chapter 2

Getting Started with Clean Architecture

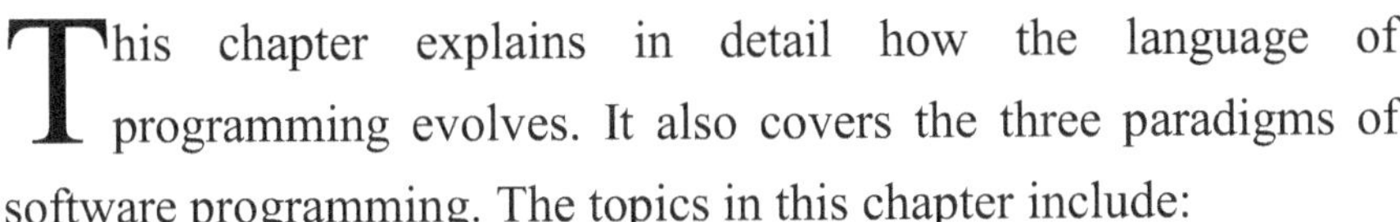

This chapter explains in detail how the language of programming evolves. It also covers the three paradigms of software programming. The topics in this chapter include:

- How the language of programming evolves

- The three paradigms of software architecture

How The Language of Programming Evolves

Every software development starts with the codes. Code is the major language of programming. The first man to lay the foundation of what we refer to as software programming today is Alan Turing, in the year 1938. Although Alan was not the first man to discover programming in computers, he was the first to find out that computer programming is simply data. Based on his realization, by 1945, he started writing real programming language in codes. His code language was binary, and his programs include loops, strings, stacks, assignments, and other functional values of software.

This development gives rise to the series of revolution in the programming language. The first among these revolutions happened in the late 1940s. Programming language evolves from the binary code introduced by Turing into assemblers. This was because of the daunting and draining task of converting programs into binary. The new language was easier to use and saves programmers from the difficulties encountered when using binary. In 1951, Grace Hopper invented AO. The main aim of AO is to compile. In fact, she coined the term *compiler* for the task the language performs. In 1953, Fortran was invented. After this, new programming languages like the COBOL, SNOBOL, C, Pascal, Java, JavaScript, ad infinitum, Scratch, and so on were invented.

Significant among these revolutions is the revolution of paradigm. In programming, the paradigm focused on how a program works. It is used to show the various elements that programming works. It tells the programmer which program structure to use and when the structure should be used. There are three paradigms in software development; they are:

- Structured programming

- Object-orient programming

- Functional programming

Structured Programming

Edsger Wybe Dijkstra discovered this in 1968. Structured programming was the first to be adopted, but not the first paradigm to be invented. In this paradigm, Dijkstra explains how the use of unrestrained jumps (**goto** statements) can be harmful to the program structure. He then replaces the jumps with blocks such as the **if/then/else** and the **do/while/until**. The major purpose of the structured programming paradigm is to impose discipline on direct transfer of control.

What led to the invention of the structured programming language was that Dijkstra discovers that programming is becoming more and more difficult to learn. The reason for this is because a program is often made up of various details extremely technical for the human brain to grasp. Also, when a programmer omits a small detail in his or her software development, the software might appear okay at the first few trials but will shut down after a while. As a result, programmers don't usually perform well in the field. To help alleviate the issue, Dijkstra introduced the structured programming that works with the mathematical discipline of *proof*. Dijkstra's aim is to use the Euclidian hierarchy of *postulates, theorems, corollaries, and lemmas*. He believes that programming will be a lot easier when programmers use this mathematical hierarchy in their program development. The hierarchy will help tie proven structures with codes so that they will prove themselves to be correct.

However, he realized that for this to work, he will have to show the technique for writing algorithms and basic proof. While carrying out his investigation, Dijkstra found out that using **goto** for some programming task prevent modules from being decomposed recursively into smaller and smaller units. As a result, the programmer can't use the divide and conquer approach necessary for proofs

Aside from the difficulty explained above, Dijkstra realized that other use of **goto** does not have this problem. But these other uses are usually simple tasks like selection, loops, iteration control structure like the **if/then/else** and **do/while**. A module that makes use of these kinds of control structures can be easily decomposed into smaller units.

It was with the knowledge of the above that Dijkstra discovered that when controls are combined with sequential execution like the mathematical hierarchy, the result will be very special. Although, this has first been discovered and proven by two renowned programmers: Bohm and Jacopini. These two programmers proved that all programs could be executed from three structures: selection, sequence, and iteration. But structured programming was shaped in such a way that the very control structure that makes a program provable we're the same one combined together to form the minimum sets of control from which programs can be built.

For the sequential statement, Dijkstra shows how this can be built by simply using the enumeration process. This mathematical approach helps trace the input of the sequence to the output of the sequence. Selection was also handled by the process of iteration, in sequence, if both the input and output produced the required mathematical result, the proof is a solid one.

However, the iteration process is a bit different. For iteration, Dijkstra introduced the use of induction. He proved the case for 1 by enumeration. He then went ahead to prove that if N is correct, then N + 1 is correct; this again uses the enumeration method.

As computer language progresses, the **goto** approach continues to dwindle while structured programming was embraced. Today, most modern programming does not have **goto**. A good example is LISP.

Functional Decomposition in Structured Programming

While explaining how structured programming work, it was revealed that with structured programming, modules could be easily decomposed into smaller. This means that structured programming allows programmers to decompose large scale modules into high-level functions. The high-level functions can be taken one by one and decomposed into a lower-level function, and the lower level function can be decomposed into smaller units. Each of the decomposed functions can then be taken and represented using the control structure of the structured programming.

As a result of this functional decomposition, disciplines such as structural analysis and structured designs became very popular, especially in the 1970 and 80s. Programmers like Ed Yourdon, Larry Constantine, Tom DeMarco, and Meilir Page-Jones were among those who made these techniques very popular and widely accepted. With the introduction of these disciplines, programmers can easily break down large modules into small provable functions.

It is the ability to show a faulty unit of modules that made structured programming a widely used paradigm today. This is also the reason why modern programmers do not support the use of unrestrained **goto** statements. At the level of software architecture development, structured programming is still considered as one of the best paradigms until this day.

Object-Orient Programming

This paradigm was discovered in 1966, two years before the discovery of the first paradigm. It came second because it was not immediately adopted. The two programmers that invented this paradigm are Ole Johan Dahl and Kristen Nygaard. These two programmers realized that the function call stack frame in the ALGOL language could be moved to a heap. When this happens, it will allow the local variables declared by a function to be still valuable long after it returns. Here is the process necessary for this to happen:

- The function will become a constructor for a class

- The local variables will become an instance variable

- The nested function becomes a method.

```
namedPoint.c
```

```c
#include "namedPoi
#include <stdlib.h

struct NamedPoint
    double x,y;
    char* name;
};
```

The process mentioned above led to the discovery of polymorphisms. Object-orient programming can be summarized as a paradigm that imposes discipline on indirect transfer of control. It works with the combination of three significant processes; inheritance, encapsulation, and polymorphism. Therefore an OO (short for object-orient) must support these three processes. Let's examine these concepts one after the other.

Encapsulation

Object-orient programming provides a very flexible and practical encapsulation of data and function. As a result of this, to carry out the encapsulation process, a line can be drawn around a cohesive set of functions and data. Outside the line, the data is hidden, and only some functions are visible. This idea is not only limited to OO, but it is also used in C programs as demonstrated below:

```
namedPoint.c
```
```c
#include "namedPoint.h"
#include <stdlib.h>

struct NamedPoint {
  double x,y;
  char* name;
};

struct NamedPoint* makeNamedPoint(double x, double y, char* name)
{
  struct NamedPoint* p = malloc(sizeof(struct NamedPoint));
  p->x = x;
  p->y = y;
  p->name = name;
  return p;
}

void setName(struct NamedPoint* np, char* name) {
  np->name = name;
}

char* getName(struct NamedPoint* np) {
  return np->name;
}
```

In the above programs, the user of **point.h** has no access to the members of the **struct Point**. The users can call the **makePoint ()** function and the **distance ()** function. This is a perfect example of encapsulation in a non-OO language.

Inheritance

This is simply the declaration of a group of variables and functions within an enclosing scope. Inheritance is also popular in C programming. However, unlike in OO language, inheritance in C programming can only be done manually. This is demonstrated in the program below:

A careful observation of the program below shows how the **NamedPoint** data structure acts as if it was derived from the **Point** data structure. This is so because the first two fields of the **NamedPoint** and the **Point** have the same structure. Aside from this, **NamedPoint** can function like **Point** because **NamedPoint** is a superset of **Point** and shares the same members ordering like **Point.**

Although this type of program has long been before the invention of OO, the inheritance program used then was mere tricky and not as detailed as what we have in OO. This type of trickery is very popular with C++, despite its popularity, its functions are convenient and elaborating as using OO programming. In OO, multiple inheritances are very easy to accomplish, but this is not possible with tricks in C++.

Indeed, OO doesn't offer something completely new; it actually made masquerading a very convenient task. In encapsulation, no point can be added to OO, in inheritance, we can add a half-point, but the most elaborated among the three processes is the last one: polymorphism.

Polymorphism

To explain polymorphism, let's take a look at the above program in C programming. In the program, the **getchar()** function reads from **STDIN** while the **putchar()** function writes to the **STDOUT**, the question that arises from these two actions is identifying the device **STDIN** and **STDOUT.** However, the function performed by the two devices is known as polymorphism.

Note: In the UNIX operating system, every IO device provides five standard functions: open, close, read, write, and seek. The signature of each of these functions is always very identical in every IO devices. The **FILE** data structure contains five pointers to function.

If STDIN is defined as a FILE and if it points to the console data structure, then the **getchar()** calls the function pointed to by the read pointer of the **file** data structured to by the **STDIN.**

From the above explanation, it can be deduced that polymorphism is an application of pointer functions. Like the two other processes, polymorphisms have long been in used before the advent of OO programming. Using a pointer to function in programming can be very dangerous. This is because, before pointers can be used to point out function, the programmer is expected to remember all the necessary convention to call out all the function through the pointer. Since the conventions are all manual, a programmer can easily forget any of the conventions. Should this happen, it creates a bug very difficult to fix.

However, to avoid this kind of, OO programming already eliminates the convention making it easy for programmers to use polymorphisms smoothly. This great advantage is something not found in C programming.

The Power Of Polymorphism

Let's assume we already created a copy program and want to use our program to copy data from the handwritten device into a speech synthesizer device. What happens to our copy program when a new IO device is created? What if changes occur? How do we change the copy program such that it works perfectly with the new program?

It is in the above dilemma that polymorphism comes in. With polymorphism, we don't need to recompile the program we already created. This is because the source code of the copy program doesn't depend on the source code of the IO device. Since the IO device can perform all the five functions already highlighted in this section, the copy program will be able to make use of all the five functions. Consequent to this, we can say that the IO device has become a plugin for the copy program.

The UNIX operating system made our copy program a plugin. The reason for this is what we all have come across. We all learned in the 1950s that our programs are *device-dependent*. The plugins architecture was invented to work with this type of program. Since the introduction of the plugin, it has been used in almost every operating system. OO made it easy for the plugin to be used anywhere with different devices.

Therefore, it can be concluded that OO programming made it possible for the programmer to gain absolute control over every source code dependency system through the use of polymorphism. With the OO device, the architect can easily create a plugin device that allows high-level modules to work independently of the low-level modules.

Functional Programming

Functional programming is a concept that started long before programming itself. This system has been in use as far back as 1930 and strongly influenced by the I-calculus invented by Alonzo Church. To explain how this works, we will use the Squares of 25 integers program. In a language similar to the Javascript, this program will be illustrated in this format.

The same program can be written in this form using the programming language Clojure. Clojure is a derivative of Lisp and also a functional program:

For those who are not too familiar with Lisp, this language might look too strong. As a result, some comments will be added to help break it down a bit. In the above program, it is obvious that **println**, **take**, **map,** and **range** are all examples of functions. Functions are called in Lisp by putting them in parentheses. This is why all the Lisp functions illustrated above are all in parentheses.

The expression (fn [x] (* xx)) written together with map is an anonymous function. It calls on the multiple functions bypassing its input argument twice or by computing with the square of its input.

To explain the whole program process, we will start from the deepest function call

- The **range** function brings back an endless list of integers beginning from 0

- Next, the endless list created by the **range** is passed to the **map** function. The **map** function then calls the anonymous squaring function on each. This action produces a new endless list of all the squares.

- After this, the list of squares is sent to **take** function. The **take** function produces a new list containing only the first 25 squares

- The action is sent to the **printin** function to print out its input. When it does, what we will have in the input is a total of 25 Square integers.

Note: the first two stages of the program created a never-ending list. However, because our main focus is to create squares of 25 integers, only the first 25 elements of the list were created. The reason for this is because, in functional programming, it is not possible to evaluate the element until it is accessed. The first 25 list was the only one accessed in our program. As a result, it was the only list evaluated and created.

Also, in explaining how the functional programming paradigm works, we make use of Clojure. There is a big difference between Clojure programming and Java programming. This difference is that Java makes use of mutable variables, while Clojure makes use of immutable variables. As a result of this, we can say that variables in functional programming do not necessarily vary. How is this possible?

Immutability And Architecture

Variables in functional programming do not necessarily vary because all the problems encountered when using multiple processors started with mutable variables. This means problems such as deadlock conditions, race condition, and concurrent conditions spring from mutable variables. None of these problems can occur when using immutable variable programming.

Since this is the case, every architect will always hope to create a software that will function smoothly in the presence of multiple threads and processors, hence immutability is advisable and works perfectly if some compromise is made. Below are the steps to using immutability.

Segregate Mutability

The first most significant compromise when using immutability is to first separate the mutable applications from the immutable ones. Once this is done, the immutable application will be able to carry out its task in a purely functional way. Also, the immutable class will be able to communicate freely with other categories that are not necessarily functional; when it does this, it allows the state of the variables to be mutable. This action is captured in the screenshot below:

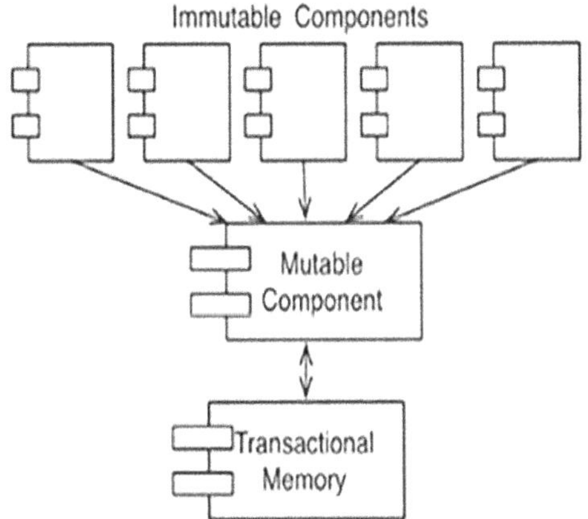

Notice the third category of the image above contains the transactional memory. This is necessary for immutability because, since the mutable state can easily cause concurrent problems in our system, it is advisable to use the transactional memory to protect the mutable variables from these problems.

The work of the transactional memory is similar to how a database is recorded on a disk. Transactional memory is used to protect the variable using the transaction or retry-based scheme.

Event Sourcing

Software storage and processing power have been receding nowadays. Today, we have processors with thousands of byte RAM and the ability to carry out unlimited instruction per. The beauty of this is that the greater the storage capacity of a system, the faster the machine works, and the lesser we need the use of mutability.

Take, for instance, the storage capacity of a banking industry system. The system is expected to be able to maintain all the account balance of its customers and also be able to mutate those account when a credit or debit transaction is carried out.

Now let's imagine that instead of carrying out the actions as explained above, the system stores only the transaction. When a customer wants to know his or her account balance, all the transactions are added up to get this. This method will require no mutability. This is the focus of event sourcing. Event sourcing is simply the process of storing only the customer's transaction without storing the statement of account. When the statement of account is needed, all the programmer needs to do is to add up the transactions. In event sourcing, the user doesn't necessarily have to wait until the customer asks for his or her statement of account. A user can update this every midnight or whenever he or she wants to. When the transaction is requested, all the users have to do is to start the task from his or her last program.

Summary

We can summarize this chapter by saying:

- Structured programming paradigm deals with direct transfer of code

- Object-orient programming paradigm deals with the indirect transfer of code

Functional programming deals with variables:

Chapter 3

Three: Principles of Design

This chapter focuses on the various principles we can use to create clean architecture. It explains in detail what the solid principle is and how this principle works. Here are the outlines that will be covered in this chapter:

- Solid principle

- Single responsibility principle

- Open-closed principle

Solid Principle

Every great software system started with clean codes. Clean codes are what we used to build the structure already mapped out by the software architect. We will use the same architecture for our house used in the first chapter of the book. Let's assume after generating a very beautiful architecture of your house, the builder started the construction with bad bricks. We will all agree that no matter how great the house looks when it is completed, it will one day crumble as a result of the bad bricks. In the same vein, assuming the bricks are okay, the design is beautiful, but the builder still made a mess of these things, our house will still not meet our taste. In programming, this is where the concept of SOLID comes in.

The principle of SOLID provides a detail explanation of how functions and can be arranged into various classes and how these classes are incorporated. The use of the word "class" does not necessarily mean that this principle is only applicable to object-orient programming. It covers all three programming paradigm. A class in this principle means a coupled grouping of data and functions. However, whether they are referred to as class or not, all software programs have these types of data grouping, and it is this type of grouping that the SOLID principle makes use of.

The Solid principle aims to create a mid-level structured program that can perform these three tasks:

- Very flexible to change

- Easy and understandable

- The basis of component that can be used in other software programs

Solid principles only apply to programmers working at the module level. The principles are appropriate for programmers working with programs just above the level of codes. The principles also to determine the kinds of software structures used within components and modules.

In our introduction, we explain that it is possible to create a messy building even with strong and valuable bricks, in the same vein, it is possible to make a mess of a system even with a well-designed mid-level component. As a result of this, this chapter and the next will extensively explain what the SOLID principle is. Next, we will move on to the other various types of principles before moving on to the principle of high-level software.

SOLID principles are made up of five broad principles. It is the first letter of each of these principles that forms the word SOLID.

- SRP: Single Responsibility Principle

- OCP: Open-Closed Principle

- LSP: Liskov Substitution Principle

- ISP: Interface Segregation Principle

- DIP: Dependency Inversion Principle

Single Responsibility Principle (SRP)

SRP is an active corollary to Conway's law. The principle states that the best structure for a software system is greatly influenced by the social structure of the organization that makes use of it. As a result, each software module has only one reason to change. As simple as this principle may sound, it is often misunderstood by programmers. This is because there is another principle similar to this one but not an SRP. The principle similar to the SRP states that a function should perform just a single task. This principle is often used for refactoring large functions into smaller ones, especially at the lower level. However, this is not an SRP principle. SRP can be explained in these three ways:

- A programmer only changes a software system to satisfy the demand of the stakeholders and users. The stakeholders and users are, therefore, the reason for the changes in the software. This fits the SRP statement that a module should only have one reason to change.

- Since the user or stakeholders are the reason for the change in a module, a module should be answerable to only one stakeholder or user. In this explanation, the word stakeholder or user does not necessarily sound appropriate. This is because, an organization can have more than one person wanting to change a module in the same way, here the change is required by a group or more than one person. Since the group wants the module to be changed into a single way, and SRP works with a stakeholder, we will replace the word stakeholder with an actor.

- From the two explanations above, we can adjust the principle by saying that a module should be responsible for one and only one actor.

What is a module?

In a very simple definition, a module is a source file used in containing codes. Although some programming language does not use module or source file to contain their code, in such programming, a module is a cohesive set of data or function. Cohesive here refers to the SRP itself. It acts like a force binding the code responsible to a single actor together. The best way to understand this principle is to look out for what happens when it is violated. There are two signs that the SRP rule has been violated; these signs include:

Accidental Duplication

To explain this sign, we will be using a program illustrating the employee's class from a payroll application. This program contains three basic information : calculatePay (), reportHours (),save ().

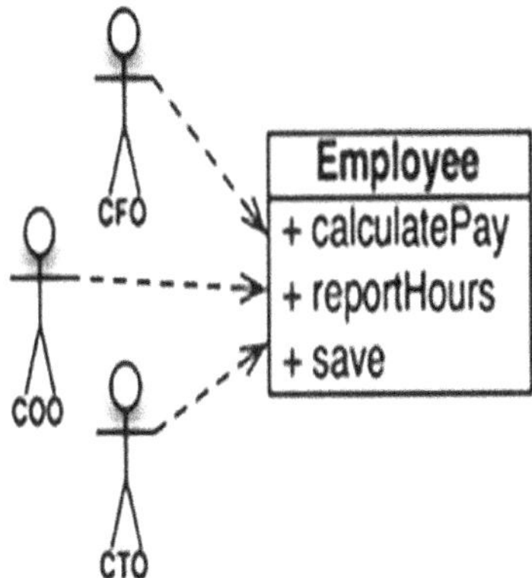

- Notice that the program above violates the SRP principle because each method in the program reports to three different actors.

- The first method, the **calculatePay ()** is controlled by the accounting department and reports to the CFO

- The second method, the **reportHours ()** is controlled by the department of human resources and reports to the COO

- The third method, the **save ()** is controlled by the database administrator and reports to the CTO

Now to rectify this, the developer can put the source code for these three classes into a single employee class. Here the developer coupled the action of the three classes into one. However, this coupling process can make the action of one affect the other. For instance, let's assume that the **calculatePay()** function and the reportHour() function use the same algorithms to calculate non-overtime hours, to avoid the imminent problems that occur when changes occur in any of the two, the developers will have to duplicate the codes and put everything in a function and then label the function: **regularHours()**. This program is captured in the screenshot below:

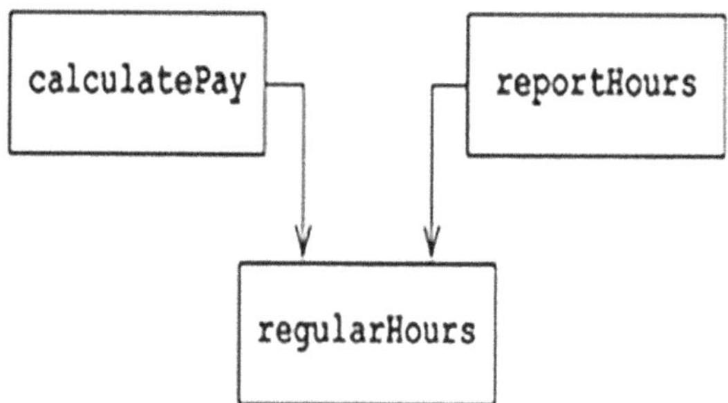

The above screenshot shows that both the calculatePay() function and the reportHour() function share the same algorithm. Let's assume that along the line, the CFO decides to make some adjustments in the way non-overtime hours are calculated. But the HR is very okay with the way the non-overtime hours works and does not any adjustment. But the CFO goes ahead to invite a developer. Unfortunately, while the developer was carrying out the task, he only noticed the **regularHours()** function called by the **calculatePay()**. He does not notice that this same function is also being called by **reportHours().** The developer makes the necessary adjustments and runs it. The CFO also checked the adjusted program, and it works as requested.

The HR is unaware of this latest development and continues to use the report generated by the reportHours() function. The numbers are incorrect, and the HR loses a huge amount of money.

The reason for the above mistake is simple. The problem occurs because the developer put the code that a different actor works within very close proximity. The principle of the SRP states that codes different actors work with should be separated.

Merge

It is not uncommon for merge problems to occur in source files that are made up of many different methods. This problem often comes up if these different methods are responsible for different actors. Using our example above, let's assume that the CTO team decides to make a little change in the employee's table of the database. At the same time, the COO team decides to make a change in the format of the overtime hours report. To do this, two different developers were invited, and they both started working separately, but along the line, their changes collided, and a merge problem occurred. Merge is a very risky problem and can even affect the third actor: CFO.

Like the accidental duplication problem, the merge problem can only be avoided by separating codes that support different actors. When the three classes are separated, the program will have three different programs. The trouble with this solution is that the developer now has three different classes to instantiate and track. The best way to do this is to use the facade method.

From our explanation so far, we can say that the Simple Responsibility Principle works with functions and classes. However, this same principle appears differently at two more levels. It becomes the Common Closure Principle at the level of component, and also becomes the Axis of Change responsible for the case of Architectural Boundaries at the level of Architectural. These different occurrences will be studied in detail in the subsequent chapter.

Open-Closed Principles

This principle was coined and made famous by Bertrand Meyer. The principle states that a software artifact should be made open for extension but closed for modification. This implies that software behavior is supposed to be made extendable without having to modify the software. This principle is the center of clean programming. If in carrying out a simple extension of some requirements in software, the developer is required to alter the modification of the software, then the software architect has done a very bad job. As a result of the importance of this principle in creating a clean architecture, it is widely recognized in programming. However, there is more to this principle, especially at the architectural level.

To explain how OCP works, we will use a thought experiment.

Thought Experiment

Let's assume that we have a system that displays the financial summary of an account on a company's webpage. On the web page, negative numbers are written in red, and the data is scrollable. Now let's assume that the stakeholder requested that the data be converted into a printable form and be printed on a black and white page. This should be carried out with the necessary details like page header, footer, margins, page breakers, and so on. The negative numbers should be made noticeable by putting them in parentheses. In carrying out this action, some new codes are required, but the problem is: How much of the old codes will need to be changed?

A very good software architect will try to reduce the old code to the barest minimum, if possible, to zero 0. To do this, the programmer will change the things for different reasons using the SRP principle already explained. Then the programmer will organize the dependencies between those things appropriately using the Dependency Inversion Principle, which will be explained in the next chapter. When we apply the SRP, in the outcome, the report will show these two process:

- the calculation of the report

- The presentation of the data into a web and printer-friendly format

When these two separations have been made, we proceed to organize the dependency of the source code. This will make it possible for changes to one not to cause changes in the other. To do this, we will partition the processes into classes and then separate each class into a component. This activity is revealed in the diagram below. Notice in the figure that the component in the upper left corner is the controller. The upper left is the Interactor; the lower right is the database, while the lower left is made up of four components representing the Presenters and the Views.

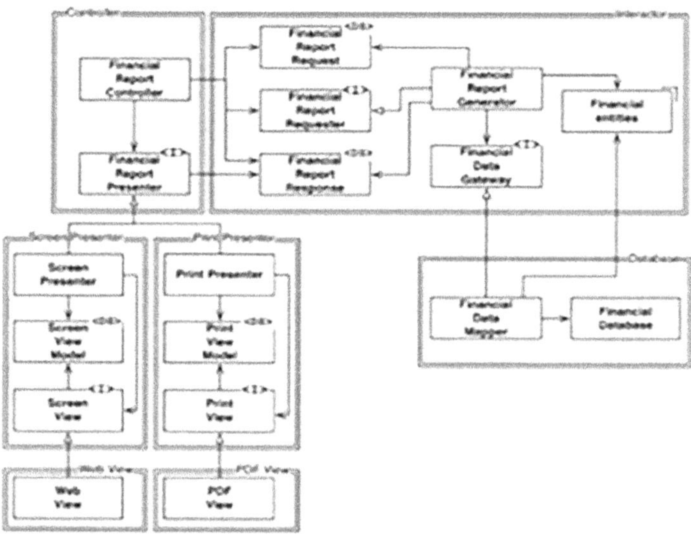

There are two important classes in the above program. The classes marked with <I> are interfaces, those marked with <DS> are data structure. The open head arrow heads using relationships while the close head arrows represent inheritance or a relationship. The first most important thing to notice with the dependencies is that they are all source code dependencies. An arrow pointing from class A to class B means that the source code of class A mentions something in class B, but the source code in class B does not mention anything in the source A. This means that the Financial DataMapper knows about Financial DataGateWay through the implemented relationship, but the Financial DataGateWay doesn't know anything about the Financial DataMapper. Another important thing to notice in this diagram is each double line is crossed in only one direction. This means that all the component relationships are unidirectional.

Summary

The Open-Closed Principle is one of the most important facets of clean architecture. It makes the system very easy to extend with the barest minimum of change. This chapter explains in detail two out of the five principles under the SOLID. The next chapter will cover the remaining three principles.:

Chapter 4

Solid Principles

Two out of the five principles under SOLID principles have been explained in the previous chapter, in this chapter, the remaining three principles will be explained:

- LSP: The Liskov Substitution Principle

- ISP: The Interface Segregation Principle

- DIP: The Dependency Inversion Principle

The Liskov Substitution Principle

Barbara Liskov developed this principle in 1988. The principle revolves around interchangeable elements. It states that to build a software programming from interchangeable parts, those parts must adhere to the agreement that these interchangeable parts can be substituted one for the other.

In explaining the principle, Barbara, who was the proponent, wrote that:

What is wanted here is something like the following substitution property: If for each object o1 of type S, there is an object o2 of type T such that for all program P defined in terms of T, the behavior of P is unchanged when o1 is substituted for o2, then S is the subtype of T

We will be using a simple illustration to explain this. Let's assume that we have a class of programs called *License*. This license class contains a *calcFee()* method used in calling the *Billing* application. The license class has two subclasses: the *BusinessLicense* and the *PersonalLicense*. These subclasses use different algorithms to calculate the license. These kinds of programs work to the rule of LSP. To function effectively, the *Billing* class does not depend on any of its two subsets. Both the two subclasses can be substituted for the license. When the LSP is violated, here are the problems that can arise from the violation.

The Square/ Rectangle problem

To understand this problem, we will be using a screenshot of a diagram showing the appearance of the problem.

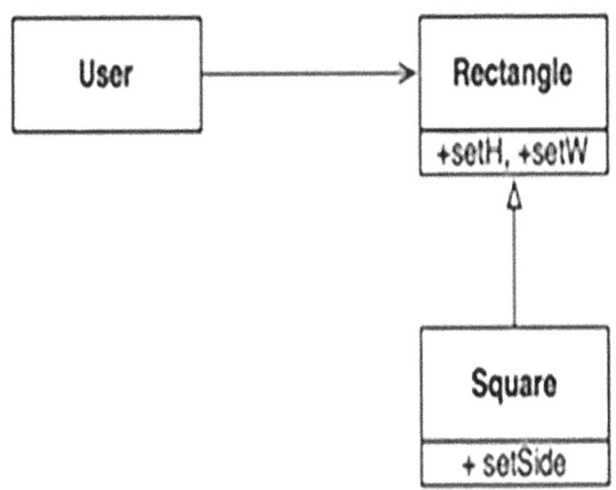

In the above program, the square is not a proper substitute for the rectangle because the height and width of the rectangle are independently mutable. In contrast to this, to conform to the principle of LSP, the height and width of the square must be changeable. Since the user of this program believes that the square is communicating with the rectangle, this can easily be confused.

The only way to rectify the problem is to add a mechanism to the user. A good example is an **if** statement. The addition of a mechanism will help confirm if the rectangle is a square.

The Interface Segregation Principle

This principle admonishes software developers to stop depending on things they don't need. It got its name from the diagram below

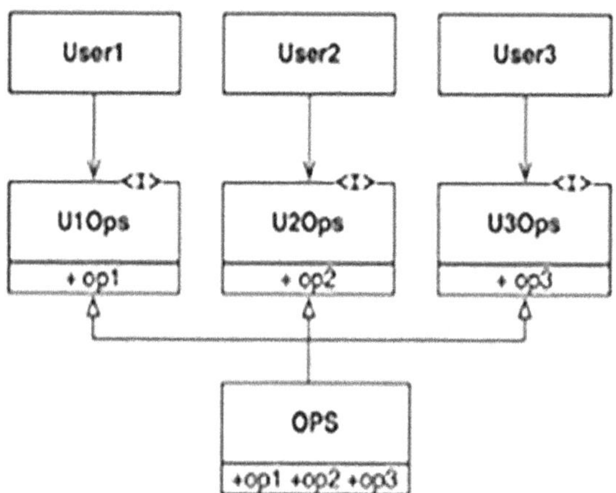

In the above program, several users are using OPS. Let's take, for instance, that user 1 uses OPS 1, user 2, OPS 2, and user 3 uses

OPS 3. The OPS program is written in Java language. This means that the source code of user 1 will also rely on OPS 2 and 3 despite not calling on them. As a result, any change in the source code of either OPS 2 or 3 will force user 1 to recompile and redeploy.

To solve this problem, we can segregate the principles, as shown in the screenshot below. If the program is still written in the Java language, the source code of user 1 will depend on u10ps and op1, but will not depend on OPS. Hence, a change in the OPS will not affect user 1 or cause it to be recompiled and redeployed.

Interface Segregation Principles and Language

From the program above, notice that the programming language affects the program. Java language forces programmers to create a declaration that must import, use, or include. The included declaration in source code creates the source code dependencies that the user to recompile and redeploy.

In other languages like Ruby and Python, these declarations do not exist. Instead, they are inferred at source time. This is the primary reason dynamically typed languages create systems that are more flexible and easy. While Ruby and Python are examples of dynamically programming language, Java is an example of statistical language.

This difference in how ISP works with program language led to the conclusion that ISP is a language issue and not an architecture issue.

The Dependency Inversion Principle

This principle states that the most flexible system are those in which source code dependencies refer only to abstraction and not to concretion. This implies that in a statistical language like Java, the source code dependencies like *use include* and *import* will only refer to source modules containing interfaces, abstract classes, or some abstract kind of declaration; no concrete modules will be depended on.

Dynamically typed languages like Ruby and Python are affected by the rule. The source code module should not include the concrete module. But in this type of language, it is a bit difficult defining what source code interface is. In simple term, source code interface will include any module in which the function being called are implemented.

However, because the string class in a programming language is always very stable and tightly controlled, software developers and architecture do not have to bother about frequently changing the modules in this program. The volatile modules of our program are those we should avoid depending on.

Stable Abstraction

Implementation is more volatile than the interface. This implies that every change to an abstract interface leads to a change in its concrete interface. However, changes to concrete implementation do not usually necessitate a change in the interfaces that are implemented. As a result, all great architects and developers try as much as possible to reduce the volatility of the interface. This they do by looking for available means to add implementation to the interfaces without affecting any changes in them.

This program implies that the stable software architecture is those that avoid depending on the volatility of the interfaces. This favors the use of stable abstract interfaces. This implication revolves around a couple of some certain coding practices:

Do not refer to volatile concrete classes instead refer to abstract interfaces. This rule cut across all languages, whether statistically or dynamically. Also, the rule avoids the creation of the object and enforce them on the use of Abstract Factories.

Do not derive from any of the volatile interfaces. This rule is deducted from the previous rule, but there is an addition. This addition is that since inheritance is very strong and stable in a statistically typed language, the dependency will also be regular. But in dynamical language, inheritance is not as strong as it is in statistically language.

Do not override concrete functions. Concrete functions usually require source code dependencies. When these functions are overridden, dependencies are not eliminated; instead, they are an inheritance. To control these dependencies, make the concrete functions abstract by adding more implementations.

Do not mention the name of anything concrete or volatile

Factory

To be able to comply with the rules mentioned above, the creation of volatile interfaces requires some specialties. Caution is very paramount because in all programming languages, to create an object, a source code dependency is required on the definition of that object.

Most object-oriented language like Java uses an Abstract Factory to manage unwanted dependencies.

The screenshot below shows the structure of the Abstract Factory.

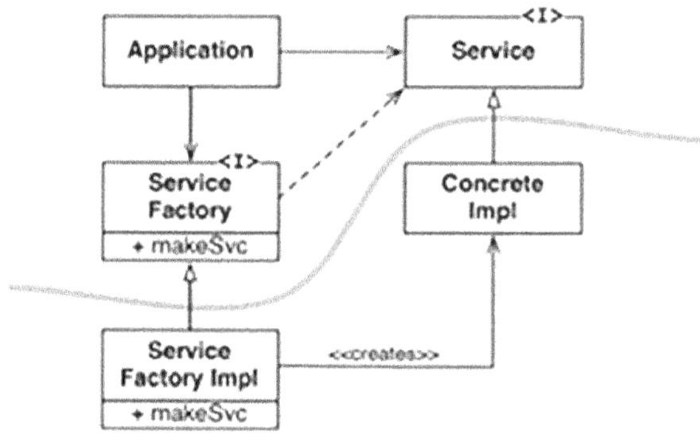

In the above program, the **Application** uses **Concrete Impl** through the **service** interface. However, the interface must somehow create instances of the **Concrete Impl** to achieve this without creating a source code on the **Concrete Impl;** the **Application** calls the **makeSvc** method of the **ServiceFactory** interface. This service is implemented by the **ServiceFactory Impl** class, which derives from **ServiceFactory.** The implementation instantiates the **Concrete Impl** and returns it to a service.

The curve line is an architectural boundary separating the concrete interfaces from the abstract. The abstract interfaces include every high-level business rules of the application, and the concrete component contains all the implementation details that those rules manipulate.

In the diagram above, note that the flow of control crosses the cross line in the opposite direction of the source code dependencies. The dependencies of the source code are inverted against the flow of control. This is why the principle is referred to as the Dependency Inversion Principle.

Concrete Component

In the image above, the concrete element contains only a single dependency, so it violates the DIP. This is quite common with dependency inversion. Violations like this cannot be rectified. They can only be gathered into a small number of concrete elements and kept separately from the system.

Summary

This chapter covers the remaining three principles under the SOLID principle, from the explanation so far, we note that to create clean software, our program must adhere to some principle. Failure to comply can lead to problems too difficult to rectify. As we progress in other principles of designs, especially the higher-levels principles, we will be using some of the principles under the SOLID. The DIP will come up again and again and become the most visible principle in architecture programs.:

Chapter 5

Component Principles

In examining the principles under SOLID, it was mentioned that all these principles only apply to bricks. They are used to arrange bricks into walls and rooms. The next principle is a buildup on the SOLID. While SOLID deals with bricks, COMPONENT principles on how to arrange rooms into a building. This explanation is in relationship to our explanation of what architecture is. The larger building is a product of smaller buildings arranged to form the big edifice.

Software Component

A component is a unit of deployment. They are the smaller entities that are used to create part of the system. The software components of some programming languages are highlighted below:

- Java programming - jar file.

- Ruby - gem files.

- Net - DLLs

In compiled languages, the software component is the aggregation of the binary data. In interpreted languages, they are the aggregations of source files. In all languages, they are a granule of deployment.

A component can be linked together to form a single executable. They can also be aggregated together into a single archive. A component can be independently used as separate dynamical plugins. Examples of these include **jar, .exe,** and **dll.** A well-developed component will always retain these two abilities:

Ability to be independently deployable

Ability to be independently developable

History of Software Component

Before the advent of components, programmers controlled the memory location and layout of their programs. Among the first line of codes that was usually used is the **origin** statement. This is used to declare the address of where the program will be loaded. A good example is the PDG -8 program illustrated below. In the program, a subroutine called GETSTR was used. This is used to implement a string from the keyboard and then input it in a string.

```
                              *200
                              TLS
START,                        CLA
                              TAD   BUFR
                              JMS   GETSTR
                              CLA
                              TAD   BUFR
                              JMS   PUTSTR
                              JMP   START
BUFR,                         3000

GETSTR,                       0
                              DCA   PTR
NXTCH,                        KSF
                              JMP   -1
                              KRB
                              DCA   I   PTR
                              TAD   I   PTR
                              AND   K177
                              ISZ   PTR
                              TAD   MCR
                              SZA
                              JMP   NXTCH

K177,                         177
MCR,                          -15
```

The ***200** at the beginning of the program tells the compiler to generate codes that will be loaded at the **200g** address. This kind of program is novel to today's programmers who do not have to bother themselves with where the program will be loaded in the memory of the computer. But in those days, programs are not relocatable.

How Library Functions are Located in Those Days

In the early days of programming, the library was saved in the source class and not in the binary. To access this, programmers will have to join the source code of the library function with the application code and then compile them as a single code.

This approach became challenging because of the limited device space. Not only this, devices in this period, was very slow, and getting a memory is very expensive. Also, as the library file grows, compilers are forced to make several passes at the source code, but as expected, the memory space became too small to keep all the source codes.

As a result of the problem, the compiler is left with no option but to read from the source code using the slow device. The longer the compiler, the longer the time spent reading from the source code. This approach is not only time consuming but also effort draining.

To control and shorten the time spent on source code, programmers separate the source code of the application function from that of the library function. Next, they created a symbol table for the function library. When they want to run an application, they will load the binary function library and then load the application function.

The solution works very well so long as the application could fit to address 0000g and 1777g. But along the line, the size of the application increases, forcing programmers to split the application into two segments around the library function.

The problem continues to grow as the size of the application increases. It becomes clear that to rectify the issue, something entirely different has to be done. This gave birth to relocatability.

Relocatability

The solution to the problem is relocatability. This approach is very simple. The programmer only has to convert the compiler into an output binary code that could be relocated in memory by a small loader. To run this, the loader will be told where to load the relocatable code. The relocatable code was instrumented with flags used to inform the loader which part of the loaded data has to be selected and loaded at the address selected.

Also, the compiler was changed to emit the names of function as metadata in the relocatable binary. If a program calls a library function, the compiler will emit the name as an **external reference**. If a program defined a library function, the compiler will emit the name as an **external definition**. Once the compiler has emitted the names of the functions called, the loader can easily link the external reference to the external definition.

This approach gave birth to **linking loaders.**

Linkers

The linker loaders allow a programmer to divide their works into small compilable, and loadable units. This works well when both programs linked together are very small. However, as programming progress, this approach begins to have its own problem. Notable among its problems is that it became too slow to work with. The larger the program, the more time the linkers take to load. It could take as long as an hour to successfully link programs.

To rectify this, the loading and the linking were separated into two phases. The slow part that did the linking was developed into an application called **Linker**. The output of the linker was a linked relocatable that a relocating loader could load very easily.

From the explanation so far, the software component is the dynamically linked file that can be plugged together at runtime. From our explanation above, it is obvious that before the component can be run in a very casual way, it took years of developing and creating new applications. The next outline will cover all aspects of component cohesion.

Component Cohesion

Here we will be examining how components are grouped into classes. Three principles are guiding the grouping of components:

REP : Reuse / Release Equivalent Principle

CCP: Common Closure Principle

CRP: Common Reuse Principle

Reuse/Release Equivalence Principle

Reuse granule is the same as the release granule.The steady advancement in programming gave rise to the birth of some managerial tools like the Maven, Leiningen, and RVM. These tools have been greatly improved. Because, during the early days of programming, a vast number of reusable components and component libraries were created. Today, we are living in the age of software reuse.

The Reuse/ Release program states that people who want to reuse a software component can only do that if the component is tracked to a release process and given a release number. Without the release numbers, there is no other way to ensure that all the reuse components are compatible with each other. Software programmers are required to know when new releases are coming and the changes the new release will bring. The release process must produce the necessary notification and release documentation. This will help the software user to know when and whether to add the new release.

Put simply, from a programmer point of view, the classes and modules that are grouped together to form a component must belong to a cohesive group. Modules cannot be taken from random classes to form a component. All modules in a component must share some intrinsic functionality.

This principle also implies that classes and modules that are grouped together must be releasable together. The fact that they share similar release numbers, names, and documentation should give some clues to the user or programmer. Violation of this principle is easy to detect and could make the developer look like an amateur.

The Common Closure Principle

This principle states that all the classes that change for the same reasons and at the same should be gathered into a component while classes that change at different times and for different reasons should be separated into different components.

A careful observation of the rule will show that it shares great similarities with the Single Responsibility Principle. The SRP states that a class should not have multiple reasons to change; CCP states that a component should not have multiple reasons to change. The only difference between the two principles is SRP applies to classes while CCP applies to a component.

Maintainability is more important than reusability in most applications. As a result, if there must be any changes in the code of an application, these changes should occur in one component rather than spreading around all the other components. When changes are limited to a single component, redeployment and recompilement will be limited to that single component. The components that are not affected does not need to be redeployed.

This principle prompts developers to gather together all the classes that are likely to change for the same reason. It is these classes that we will use to form our component.

The Common Reuse Principle

The principle states that do not force users of a component to depend on things they don't need

This is another principle that helps us to determine which class of modules to form a component. It states that classes and modules that will be reuse together should belong to the same component. Classes are usually not reused in isolation. Since CRP states that this type of class belongs to the same component, it is expected to see modules that have lots of dependencies on each other in a component.

Tension Resulting from Component Cohesion

From the brief explanation of these three component principles, it is obvious that these three principles counter one another and will tend to fight in a program. The first two principles, the REP and the CCP are all-inclusive while the last CRP is an exclusive principle. The inclusive principles are so because from their approaches, they tend to make a component larger while the exclusive one makes a component smaller.

As a result of the tension between these principles, developers who focus on any of the three will face some difficulties. For instance, focusing on the REP and CRP will affect too many components when any changes are made, in the same vein, focusing on the CCP and REP will produce too many unneeded resources.

To rectify this, the architect will have to find a point of agreement among all three principles. This position will also meet the stakeholders or users requirements

Summary

Having explained all three principles of component cohesion, it can be summarized that all three principles explain a complex variety of cohesion. To choose the classes or modules to form components, the architect should take note of reusability and readability. These two factors must be well balanced in a component:

Chapter 6

Component Coupling

This chapter will focus on the next three principles of software components. These principles focus on the relationship between components. In our explanation, we will also be expatiating on the tension between components, as seen in the previous chapter. We will explain the three forces that impinge on the architecture of a component structure. These forces include: political, technical, and volatility. This chapter will cover:

- Acyclic dependencies principles

- How cycle affects a component

- Breaking the circle

- Stability in a software component

- How to measure stability

- Stability abstraction principle.

The Acyclic Dependencies Principles

This principle allows no cycles in the component dependency principle. To explain how it works, let's take some moment to think back to the time we have already completed some things in our software. All the programs are working fine before we shut down our systems and close for the day. Unfortunately, when we came back the next day, we are greeted by faulty programs and wonder how this happens. It is not uncommon for us to face a situation similar to this, especially when working with a team of software developers. The reason for this is simple: someone in the team has tampered with your stuff and changed some of your programs.

This type of problem can keep evolving, especially when working with a large team of developers. However, some decades ago, the telecommunication industry came up with two solutions to this problem. They are the Weekly Build, and the Acyclic Dependencies Principle commonly referred to as ADP.

The Weekly Build

This solution is very common with average-sized projects. This solution works as the name implies, all the developers in the team are to work independently for the first four days in the week. On the fifth day, they integrate their works together and build their change. The approach offers a splendid opportunity for developers to work on private copies of codes for the first four days. However, the disadvantage is usually on the workload on the fifth day. Except for this, the approach is very okay.

One major factor that causes the disadvantage is the size of the program. As the size of the program increases, integrating becomes more difficult to achieve in a day. It sometimes spills on the second day. In the long run, some managers might suggest running the program bi-week. This also gets more difficult to work with as the programs increasing. This situation eventually leads to a crisis. Integrating becomes harder to achieve, and the developers are frustrated.

The solution to this is simple. The best way to go about it is to partition the development component into releasable components. Once the component is partitioned into releasable components, they become easy for the team of developers to work with. When a unit or component is found working, the developer releases it to other members of the team. Each member of the team must modify this independently.

When another release is made available, all the developers in the team decides on when to adopt it. If they all decide not to work with the new release yet, they simply continue with the old one. This solution is very simple and easy to work with. However, the problem with this is that there can be no cycle in the dependency structure when this is violated; it can lead to the problem we want to avoid at the onset. The image below delineates this:

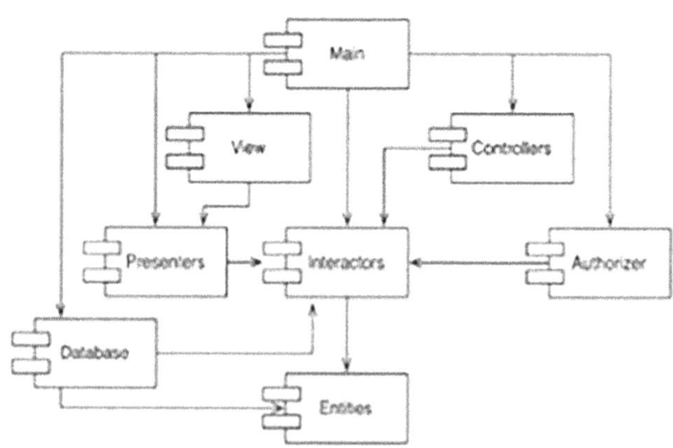

In the above diagram, the nodes are the components, while the directed edges are the dependency structure. In the program, irrespective of the structure you choose to work with, there are no cycles. This structure is a Directed Acyclic Graph (DAG).

Let's assume in the above program, the Presenter team decided to produce a new release. The team that will be affected by the release is the Main and View. This is because they are the two next team when we follow our dependency arrow backward. Thus when a new release is to be initiated by the Presenter team, the three teams will have to come together to agree on when to start using the new release.

However, when the Main team releases a new change, no team is affected because the Main class has no team dependent on it. Hence, the impact of the Main team on other teams is relatively small.

How A Cycle Affects the Component Dependency

Let's assume that in the program above, a new requirement is to be made in the **Entities** class. This should be done in such a way that the new requirements will also be used in the **Authorizer**. This action cannot be carried out without using a dependency cycle.

The developer working with the Database class is aware that for the new requirements to be released, it must be harmonious with the **Entities** class and the **Authorizer** class.But the **Authorizer** in this program also depends on the **Interactor**. This complication makes it very difficult for the database to release new requirements without affecting all the other teams. How then do we fix this problem?

Breaking The Cycle

There are two major ways to carry out this exercise

For the situation explained above, here are the steps to apply the DIP

- Create an interface with the exact methods needed by the user.

- Insert the method into user, then set the **Authorizer** to inherit the interface

- The two steps above will invert the dependency between the Authorizer and the Entities, thereby breaking the cycle.

- Creating a New Component

- Create a new component in which both the **Authorizer** and the **Entities** depend on

- Move the class that the two application depends on to the component just created.

The Stable Dependencies Principles

This principle works with the direction of stability. The principle argues that a design cannot be created in a static way. There must be some volatility if the design is to be preserved. There is a conformation between this principle and the Component Closure Principle (CCP) treated in the previous chapter. For our designs to meet the standard of this principle, our components must be created in a way that they are sensitive to some changes and immune to others. This implies that the component we want to be volatile must not be dependent on one that is too hard to change. If this is ignored, the volatile component will also be hard to change.

What Is Stability in Software Development?

The stability of any software component is directly related to the amount of time it takes to make any changes in the component. Among the factors that usually make software difficult to change are its clarity, size, and complexity. However, our focus is on the most notable way to make a component difficult to change. This is by making too many components dependent on it. This situation has already been explained in the previous principle. A component that has too many dependencies is stable because it required a lot of effort to make any changes in it. The diagrams below expatriates on how a stable component works.

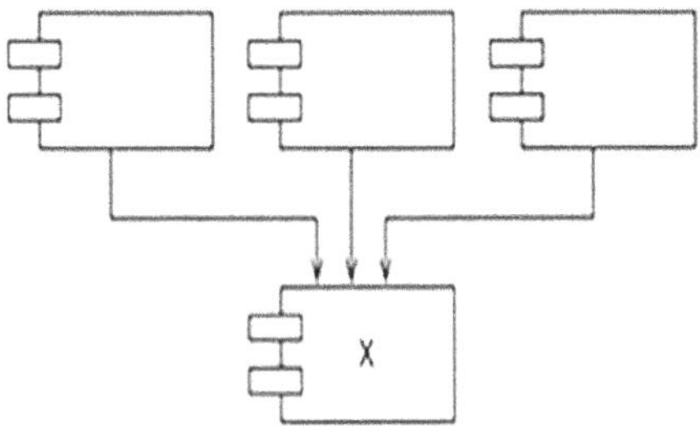

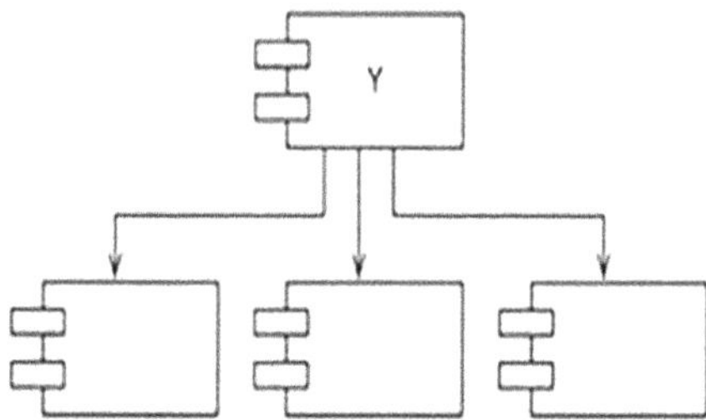

Let's consider the two diagrams above. Notice that for the **x** diagram, there are three components dependent on it, while **x** itself does not depend on any of these components. For its dependency ability, **x** is **responsible** for the three components. However, for its ability not to depend on any component, **x** is **independent.** Thus, **x** is a **stable component**

Unlike the **x** diagram, **y** is very different. No components are depending on **y,** but **y** itself is dependent on three components. For its dependency on other components, **y** is **dependent,** for its lack of component depending on it, **y** is **irresponsible.** Thus **y** is an **unstable component.**

How to Measure the Stability of a Component

The easiest way to do this is to count the number of components that comes in and out of the component. There are three metrics used to carry out this action: they are:

- *Fan-Out.* This represents outgoing dependencies. The metric is used in identifying the number of classes inside the component that depend on classes outside the component.

- *Fan-in*. This represents incoming dependencies. The metric is used in identifying the number of classes outside this component that depend on classes within the component.

- *I*: Instability. The equation for *I* in this metric is $I = Fan\text{-}In + Fan\text{-}Out$. The range for this metric is [0,1]. *I*=0 is used to represent a maximally stable component, while *I*=1 is used to represent a maximally unstable component.

To calculate the *Fan-In* and *Fan-Out* metric, we simply count the number of components outside the program we are working with that have dependencies with the classes of components inside the program we are working with.

Programs like C++ and Java have names used to identify these dependencies. In C++, the dependencies are represented with *#include* statements. When all the source codes have been sorted out into a class such that we have classes representing each source code, the I metric becomes very easy to calculate. In Java, we can calculate the *I:* instability by the *import* statements and qualified names.

When the sum of the *I* metric is 1, it means there is no component depending on this component (*Fan-In*=0), and this component depends on other components (*Fan-Out>0*). In this calculation, the program is maximally unstable, dependent, and irresponsible. Because of its lack of dependencies, the component has no reason not to change.

However, when the sum of the *I* metric is 0, it means the component is depended on by other components (*Fan-In*>0), but the component itself does not depend on any of the other components (Fan-Out=0). This type of component is maximally stable, independent and responsible. In succinct, the dependency ability of this component makes it hard to change, since it has no dependencies that might help initiate the changes.

Stable Dependency Principle states that the *I* metric of a component must be greater than the *I* metric of the components that it depends upon.

However, it is important to note that when creating your software component, not all the components should be maximally stable. If this occurred, it will make changes impossible. The software component should be a blend of both stable and unstable components.

The Stable Abstraction Principle (Sap)

This principle states that a stable component should be abstract. The first question that arises from this principle is, where do we put the high-level component? The simple way to arrange the high-level components is by creating software that does not require constant changes. The high-level software component should be positioned in the stable component (1=0); volatile software should be made up of unstable component (1=1). This will help make it very easy to change.

SAP maintains that there should be a relationship between abstractness and stability. All stable components must also be abstract. The abstractness quality will help make it easily extendable. However, abstractness is not required for unstable components; rather, all unstable component is expected to be concrete. The concrete feature will make it very flexible to change.

The combination of SAP and SDP amounts to the DIP for a component. This statement is true because the SDP can be summed up as all dependencies components should be stable. SAP can also be summed up as all stable components must also be abstract; these two statements can be summed up to mean that dependency run in the direction of abstraction.

How to Measure Abstraction

The measurement of the abstractness of a component is represented by the letter **A**. **A** is calculated by dividing the ratio of the interfaces and abstract classes in a component to the overall number of components we have in the class. The equation is summarized below:

$$A = Na \div Nc$$

Na = the number of abstract classes and interface in a component

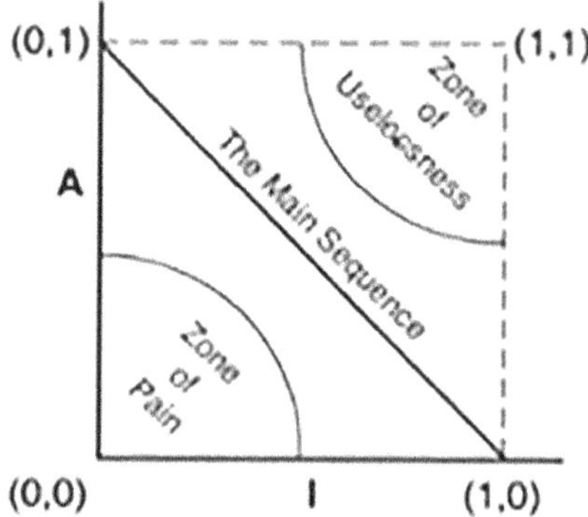

Nc = the number of classes in a component

The ranger for the A metric is 0 to 1. When the value is 0, it means the component does not have an abstract class. But when the value is 1, it means the component is made up of only abstract classes.

How To Measure The Relationship Between Stability (I) And Abstractness (A)

We will be plotting a graph to explain this relationship. The (I) is located at the horizontal axis while (A) is on the vertical axis. The maximally stable and abstract component is fixed at the upper left (0,1) while the maximally unstable is at the lower right (1,0)

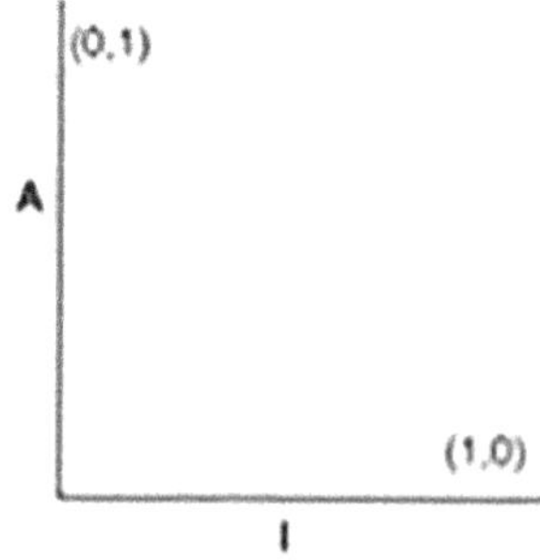

It is noteworthy that in defining the relationship between stability and abstractness, not all components will be one of the two. This is because components have varying degrees of abstractness or stability. Since there is no rule to determine the level of either of the two features in a component, we will use a locus of point in our graph.

The zone of pain is the area around the (0,0). Software found in this area includes the database schema and library source. These two components are one of the most volatile components of the software system. This is one of the major reasons why creating any change in the database schema is always very difficult. Although the library source falls within the volatile component, it's actually not volatile. A non-volatile component is not harmful and is not likely to change.

Summary

This chapter covered all the remaining three components of the software. It examines how a component is made to be dependent on another component. The chapter also examines how stability and abstraction are determined in a component, how these two features are measured, and the effect of the two features in a component:

Chapter 7

Architecture

The next seven chapters of this book explain architecture in detail. This chapter covers the following

- Who is a Software Architect, and what is the duty of a software architect?

- Explanation of the functions of the software architecture

- Decoupling layers, use case and mode

- How to decouple mode

The simplest definition for a software architect is a programmer. All software architects are programmers, and they do the works of programmers. Their works center on creating a design that is both flexible and very productive. They don't stop working with codes. Although they may not work with codes as much as other programmers, they don't stop taking programming tasks.

What Is A Software Architect?

The architect of software is the structures and layouts given to the software. The software architect is the one who designs this layout.

The architect works on how the structure of the software is divided into components, how the components are arranged, and how the components are structured to communicate with each other.

The main aim of the software architect is to simplify the operation, functionality, and maintenance of the components that make up the software. It is important to note that the layout of software does not play any role in the functionality of the software. We have a lot of systems today with outrageous shapes and structures, but whose level of productivity is unbeatable. This does not imply that the architect does not play any role in the functionality of a software; it does. But its role is more passive than active.

The function of a software architect includes:

- Ensure the system is very simple to understand and operate

- Ensure the system is easy to develop and deploy

- Ensure the system is easy to maintain

Functions Of A Software Architecture

Development

When a software system becomes too difficult to develop, it might affect the durability of the system. Hence, it is the job of the architect to ensure that the software is easy to develop by the team working with it. The team of developers usually influences the decision on how best to make a software manageable. For instance, a small team of five developers can easily work and develop a monolithic system that does not have an explicit interface or component. It is even possible for such a team to find the structure of the software as a hindrance to developing it. This accounts for why many software is with ludicrous architecture. It is from the development importance of software that Conway's law springs up. The law states that *"any organization that design a system will produce a design whose structure is a copy of the organization's communications structure."*

However, let's assume each of the five teams of developers has seven developers working under it; the development process will require that the layout of the system is well-defined and well-detailed.

Deployment

The deployment ability of software determines the effectiveness of that software. The higher the cost of deployment, the lesser the use of that software. The aim of the software architect should be to ensure the structure of the system is designed in such a way that it can be deployed with a single action. Unfortunately, developers seldom pay attention to this aspect. It is not uncommon for developers to use a micro-service architecture. At the initial stage, this approach makes the system very easy to develop. But when it comes to deploying the system, it becomes a very difficult task.

Operation

The extent the structure of software affects its operation is very minimum. When software becomes difficult to operate, this can be rectified by adding more hardware to the system and not by making any changes in the structure. The contribution of the architect to the operation of the system is to ensure that the layout of the operation is obvious to the developers. If the system is expected to handle a thousand work per hour, the architect must ensure the layout of the system will allow this kind of operation.

Maintenance

This is the most expensive aspect of the software. The endless need for correction, adding, and trails of defect a lot of human resources. The primary cost of maintaining a system falls into two categories: spelunking and risk. Spelunking is the price of uncovering existing software while trying to determine the best position or strategy to fix in new features or mend the damage.

Decoupling Layers, Uses, And Modes

From our explanation, it is quite clear that the job of the architect does not influence the behavior of the system; rather, the structure of the system. However, this does not mean that the architect does not contribute to the effectiveness of software behavior. The architect ensures that the behavior of the system is clearly mapped out and accurately specified for the developer to work with. The developer does not have to start looking for how the software is expected to behave; this aspect is already made visible at the top-level of the system by the architect.

Let's consider the use case of the system and assume the architect does not have a solid foundation of what the use case entails. All he or she knows is that the system is for shopping. With this little information, the architect can use the SRP and CCP already explained in this book to separate the components that change for the same reason from those that for different reasons. This process is what is known as the decoupling layers' process.

There are a few classes for different reasons. Notable among these classes is the user interface. The Users Interface usually change for reasons not associated with the business rules. As a result, a good architect will ensure the UI and the Business rules are separated such that they can change independently of each other. Business rules are usually closely tied to the application and the domain. But the application business rule and domain rules might require unrelated changes. As a result, these two types of rule should be separated from each other, so that changes in one does not create changes in the other.

The query language, database, and schema are also classes that changed independently. The architect is expected to separate them from one another.

Another thing that changes for different reasons is the **use case**. For instance, the use case for adding more entries to order will constantly change for different reasons and purposes than a use case for deleting an order from a program. The use case is the thin vertical slice that cut through the horizontal layer of a system. For every use case, there is a separate User Interface, application rule, business rule, and database functionality. The architect is expected to separate both the horizontal layer and the vertical layer.

In decoupling the use case of the system, each are separated from the other. The use case for adding is also separated from the one used for deleting. When this action is effectively carried out, changes in one will not affect the other.

The last decoupling, we will be considering is the mode decoupling. Each of the other two types of decoupling affects the mode of the system. When we separate the use case of the software system, we have inadvertently separated the classes that run at high throughput from those that run at low throughput. When the database is separated from the UI, then it can be run separately on different servers. Since the model of a system is the operation of that system, any changes in the uses case is also a change in the operation of the system.

How to Use the Decouple Mode

There are three ways to use the decoupling mode in a software system.

- Decoupling at the level of source code

- Service or execution decoupling

- Deployment or binary code decoupling

Source Code Decoupling

The source code decoupling is commonly referred to as a monolithic structure. This type of decoupling happens when the component is executed in the same address space and communicate with each other using simple function calls. The changes in the source code can be controlled in such a way that changes in one does not affect changes in any of the other source codes, for instance, RubyGem.

Deployment Code Decoupling

In deployment decoupling, the architect controls the dependencies between deployable units so that changes in the source code of one module does not influence changes in any of the module.

Service Code Decoupling

Here, the dependencies are reduced to the level of data structure. Communication among the components is solely through network packages such that every execution unit is entirely independent of source and binary changes in others.

Summary

This chapter explains in detail who a software architect is and the job of a software architect. The chapter also examines the decoupling methods we have in software architecture. The next chapter will explain the process involved in creating a software architecture.

Chapter 8

Drawing Lines

This chapter examines the first process of designing a clean architecture. We will be using the rules and all the explanation so far in creating our software. The chapter explains the following topics:

- Drawing lines

- Input and output of a system

- Plugin Architecture

- Boundary anatomy

Software architecture focuses more on drawing lines. In programming, these lines are referred to as boundaries. The boundaries are what the architect use in separating one software element from the other. They are also used to restrain a component of software elements from depending on other components. Boundaries are used to separate components dependencies. Usually, the architect starts his design by drawing out the lines that will be used in the system. However, there is no rule stating that designs should be started in this format. Lines can also be created at the end of the system structure. The boundaries drawn at the beginning of the software are used for deferring decisions and for keeping these decisions from affecting the essence of the system.

In the previous chapter, it was established that the goal of software architecture is to ensure that the human resources needed to keep a system is minimized to the barest minimum. The architect will also ensure that the software system is flexible enough for changes. High cost of maintenance usually occurs when systems are coupled with premature decisions. Premature decisions are decisions that have nothing to do with the business requirements of the system; examples are decisions of utility library, framework, web server, database, and so on. The validity of software is determined if decisions like the above mentioned are made deferrable.

How To Determine The Lines To Draw And When To Draw The Lines

As already explained above, lines are to be drawn on both the things that matter to the effectiveness of the system and things that don't. For instance, the Graphic User Interface does not matter to the system's business. Hence lines should be drawn on it, the database does not also matter to the GUI and the business rules, but the line should also be drawn on it.

Most often than not, we have been taught that the database is very important to the business rule, but this is misguided information. As explained in the previous chapter, the business only make use of the database indirectly. This means that the database does not need to know about the query language or the schema and other information contained in the database. All the business rule makes use of are the sets of information used to save and fetch data. As a result, we put the database behind the business rule in our system.

Where Do We Fix our Boundary Line?

The boundary line is usually below the database, just across the inheritance relationship. This diagram below captured this.

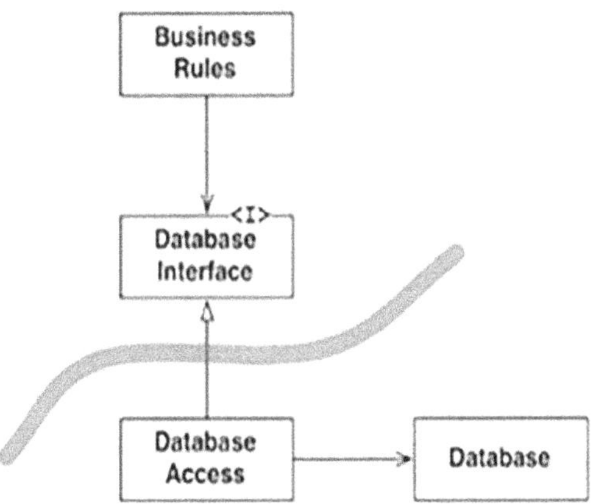

In this diagram, we note that two arrows are leaving the DatabaseAccess class. Each of these arrows points away from the DatabaseAccess. This means none of these two arrows are aware of the existence of the DatabascAcccss. The second diagram below shows how a line is cut through the database and the business rules.

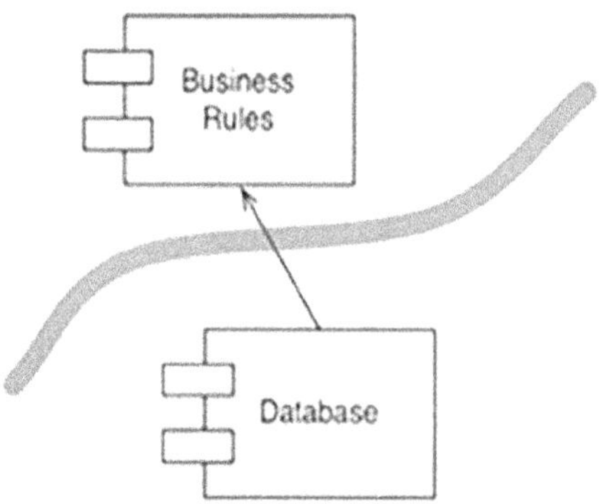

In the diagram above, we will observe similar occurrences like the first diagram. The database knows about the BusinessRule, but the BusinessRule does not know about the Database. This can be interpreted as the Database Interface exists inside the BusinessRule while the DatabaseAccess class lives in the Database. The interpretation of this validates the assertion that the BusinessRule only makes indirect use of the Database. The direction of the line in the diagram implies that the Database is not important to the BusinessRule, but the Database itself cannot exist or function outside the BusinessRule.

The Database has the code that translates the code made by the BusinessRule into the query language of the database. It is this code used for translation purposes that knows about the BusinessRule.

From the explanation of our diagram, we now know that the business rule can make use of any database. The changes or replacement made in the database does not affect the fhd database. This implies that the decisions of the database can be deferred. The database can use different implementations like the Oracle, Couch, MySQL; this will not affect the business rule.

The Input and Output Of A System

The most common definition of a system, especially by developers and business managers, is the system is the same as the GUI. Based on this misguided information, developers and business managers think the GUI initiates the work of the system. However, there is a principle guiding the input and output of a system. This principle is that IO is irrelevant. The behavior of the IO is not the behavior of the system.

Let's take the video game as an example. In using the video game, what we usually pay attention to are the mouse, the screen, the sound of the game, and the interface. We ignore the most vital component of the video game, the set of data structures and functions driving the interface. The system does not need the interface for it to carry out its function; it can execute all its functions without the game being displayed on the screen. This analogy applies to higher systems. Like the database, the interface does not matter to the business rule.

The Plugin Architecture

Software Development concentrates on how to create a software plugin that enables scalable and maintainable software architecture. A plugin in which the basic business rules are separated from those components that are optional and can be implemented in different forms.

Let's assume in building our software, we decide to make the database and user interface a plugin. This means we can plug in different kinds of user interfaces like the Web-based, SOA based, and many more. For the database, we can replace it with any other database like NoSQL, SQL or a system-based database.

In the initial creation of our web-based, making a replacement will not be difficult, but writing the plugins for the client-server User Interface might be challenging. Some of the communication between the new user interface and the business rule might have to be reworked.

In designing our plugins, we will select the module we want to depend on each other from those we don't want to. For instance, we don't want the business rule to be affected when changes are made in some parts of the systems, and so we select and separate this group. Also, we don't want changes in some parts to create changes in unrelated parts of the system. As a result, we arrange our systems into plugins. This helps to create firewalls that impede the propagation of changes. This will work in such a way that when, for instance, the GUI is plugged into the business rule, changes in the GUI will not create any change in the database.

This brings us to the assertion that boundaries in software architecture are drawn where there is an axis of change. The component of elements on one side of the boundaries changes at different times and for different reasons from the component at the other side of the boundary. For instance, business rule changes for different reasons and at different times, so there should be a boundary between the business rule and the GUI. Similarly, GUI, as a dependency element, changes for different reasons and at different times, so there should be a boundary between it and the business rule.

The explanation of the plugin above reinforced the Simple Dependencies Rules.

Boundary Anatomy

The boundaries of a software system differs in form and size. Below is the explanation of some sizes we have in the software boundary.

Boundary Crossing

To create a boundary-crossing, all the architect needs is to manage the source code dependencies. Boundary crossing is a way of creating a software boundary such that the functions on one side of the boundary calls on those at the other side and pass along some data. Here, source code determines the effectiveness of our boundary-crossing because changes in the source code of a component will make other source codes to be changed, recompiled, and then redeployed. Boundaries emphasized on controlling and building firewalls against these changes.

The Dreaded Monolith

The commonest and easiest software architecture has no strict physical appearance. This is simply an effective separation of data and function within a single address space and a single processor. This process is referred to as source code decoupling in our last chapter. Examining this process from the deployment standpoint is what is referred to as Monolith - a single executable file. The file can be a statistically linked C or C++ file or an executable Java file.

It is noteworthy that the invisibility of our boundaries, while the deployment process of our monolithic is ongoing, does not mean that the boundaries are not present. This type of architecture usually depend on some dynamic polymorphism to control their internal dependencies. This is the reason why object-orient development is one of the most sought after these days. Without the use of OO or some other forms of polymorphism, the architect might fall back on the use of pointers to functions to achieve their decoupling goals.

Calls from a low-level function to a high level is the easiest form of boundary-crossing. In this kind of approach, both the compile-time dependency and the run time dependency point to the direction towards the higher level. Dynamic polymorphism is used when the high level wants to invoke a service to the low level.

In monolithic, communication is always very easy and less expensive. In the same vein, communication across source codes are usually very interacting.

Deployment Components

Dynamically linked boundaries such as the Java jar file, Net DLL, Ruby Gem are the simplest physical representation of architectural boundaries. Deployment is carried out by delivering components in some binary or some equivalent deployable forms. This process does not involve the use of compilation. Deployment entails the gathering deployable units into some convenient forms.

Communication across the deployment component is similar to that of the monolithic. It is inexpensive and interactive.

Threads.

Both deployment component and monolith makes use of threads to carry out their activities. Threads are a way to group or organize a schedule and order of execution. It is neither an architectural boundary or a unit of deployment.

Local Process

The local process is a very strong boundary in software architecture. It is created by using the command line or other similar system call. The local process runs in the same set of processors as the multicore but uses a separate address space. This is because using the same address space is prevented by the memory protection. It communicate with other component using socket or other form of system communication like the mailbox.

Local processes can be a dynamically linked deployment component or a monolithic linked component. In the monolithic deployment component, various monolithic processes will have the same components compiles and linked together with them, while in the dynamically linked deployment component, the component may share the same dynamic linked component.

In the local process, the source code of the higher up process will not entail the names, lookup key, or physical addresses of the lower up process. Communication in the local process is carried out using the operating system calls, Interprocess context switches, and data marshaling and decoding. These applications are usually very easy to maintain and inexpensive.

Services

Services are the strongest boundary in a software architect. Service process starts from the command line, or other equivalent system Services does not concern itself with the physical area of the software components. Two services communicating together may not operate in the same physical processor or multicore. However, communication across service boundaries are usually very slow in comparison to function calls. The times for turnabout can take up to tens of milliseconds to seconds.

Summary

This chapter explains in detail what boundary in software architect is. It also explains all the different types of boundaries we have, ranging from the simplest to the strongest. We also linked our explanation of some of the boundaries to the decoupling processes we already explained in the previous chapter. The next chapter focus on the three basic elements of a software component.

Chapter 9

Elements of Software Architecture

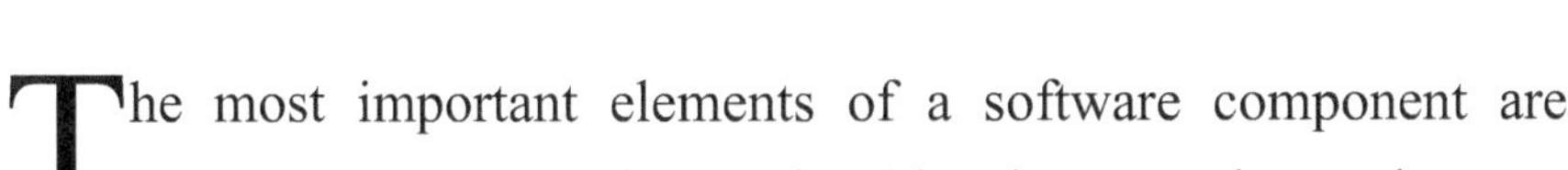

The most important elements of a software component are highlighted and explained in this chapter. These elements include:

- Policy

- Level

- Business rules

- Entities

- Use case

- Response and request models

Policy

At the heart of any software system are policies describing what the system is all about, the use, and functionality. However, these policies differ in size and structure. Some are smaller and straight to the point; others are larger and well-detailed. Whether small or large, software systems are statements of policy.

The simplest system is usually written in this format:

the overall policy of the system is divided into smaller policies.

The policy guiding the business rule is separated from that of the database or GUI.

All these divisions guide the user on how to transform input to output.

Among the important ways of building good software, software architect should ensure he or she separates the smaller policies from the larger ones, separates the policies that applied to one component from those that applied to the other, and separates policies that might be subjected to change from those that might not. Policies that change for the same reasons and at different times should be separated from those that do not.

In designing good software architecture, the regrouped component is formed into a directed acyclic graph. Policies at the same level are grouped into a component using the nodes of the graph. The direct edges form the dependencies between components. The direct edge is used to connect components that are at different levels.

In every good software architecture, the direction of these dependencies hinge upon the level of the component they are connected to. Most times, the low-level dependencies are designed to rely upon the high-level dependencies. These dependencies are source codes and compile-time dependencies.

Level

The level is simply the distance between the input and output of a software system. The extent of the level of a system is determined by the distance between the policies guiding the low-level components and the high-level component. The farther the policies of the low level from the high level, the higher their level. The policies guiding the input and output of a system are the lowest kind of policies.

Business Rules

In a simple definition, these are the rules that help determine the profits made from the software system. They are the rules used to make or save the business money irrespective of whether they are saved on the computer system or saved manually. For instance, the additional charges given by a bank on a loan is a business rule. How the bank chooses to save this money does not matter.

Business rules are very critical to the software system; they usually determine the productivity of the system. They are the rules guiding the need for the software itself. It is this aspect that stakeholders and business managers are concerned with. This is why they are sometimes referred to as critical business rules. Critical business rules will exist whether or not there is a system to automate them. However, they often require some data to work with. Our bank loan example will require the interest rate data, loan balance data, and payment schedule data to work with. These data are referred to as Critical Business Data. These rules exist whether or not the system is automated or manual. Both critical rule and critical data are mutually dependent. In programming, the combination of these two is referred to as Entities.

Entities

This is the object embedded in our computer system containing part of the critical business rules operating on the critical business data. The Critical business data is enclosed in the entities, or the entities are given free access to these data. For instance, our Bank loan example will contain three-piece of Critical Business rules: principle guiding the loan process, rate or amount of money required, and period of the loan. Each of these three-piece rules represents a class.

When we build a class like this in our system, we have successfully separated the software that implements the critical business rule from the others in the system we are building. The class we have created stands as a representative of the business. It has no business with the user interface, database, or third party framework. It works for the business irrespective of how the system was presented or the data was stored. The entity is strictly for business purpose and nothing more or less.

To create an entity, all you have to do is to bind Critical Business rule and the Critical Business data together into a single and separate software module.

Use Cases

There is some business rule that is not as pure as the **Entities**. This type of business rule defined and determined the way an automated system is used in other to save and make money for the business. This type of rule cannot be used manually; they only work with an automated system. Using our bank loan as an example, the bank officers might decide that for anyone to be qualified for a loan, he or she must have a piece of valid contact information and credit balance above 30,000 nairas. As a result, all this information must be validated before the implementation of the loan. To avoid compromising this standard, the bank specifies the condition on the system. This example is a **Use Case**. It described the way the bank loan data is used. The bank loan data here is a Critical Business data and also an automated one.

A use case can, therefore, be defined as an automated system that specifies requirements such as the input to be provided by the user, the processing steps for the output to be returned to the user. A use case defines application-specific business rules against the Critical Business Rules within the Entities.

The use case involves the rules guiding when the Critical Business rules should be initiated and how the rules are to be initiated. It does not have any business with the user interface but indirectly specifies the data coming in and out of the interface. The use case cannot determine where the application is to be delivered from, whether on the web, the console, or on the thick client. They do not describe the application to the user; rather, they focus on the application-specific rules governing the interaction between the user and the Entities. The use case does not describe the input and output of the data.

The use case is an object with one or more functions used to implement the application-specific rules. It entails the data elements needed to implement the input data, the output data, and the appropriate entities with which these data interact.

Entities are not aware of the use case that controls them. This assertion echoes the Dependency Inversion rules for high-level components. Entities are a very good example of the high-level component, while the use case is an example of a low-level component. The low level is aware of the high-level components, but the high level is not aware of the low-level components or its influence upon it.

Reasons why Entities are High Level while Use Case is Low-Level

Entities are high level because they belong to the components that can be used to call different applications; hence they are far away from the input and output of the system. However, the use case is specific to a single application. As a result, they are very close to the input and output of the system. Entities do not depend on the use case, but use case depends on entities.

Response and Request Models

The use case is very close to the output and input of a system. It expects the input and uses this to produce the output. However, a good use case should not have any connection with the way the data is communicated to the user or to any other component of the software system. Our code within the use class should have no business with the SQL or HTML.

The request data accepted by the use case for the input process and the output are not dependent on anything. This absent of dependencies is essential. If the request and response models are not independent, the use case that works with them will be inadvertently bound to the component any of these two depends on.

Summary

Of the three aspects explained in this chapter, the business rule is much more important. It is the main reason for the existence of the software system. They determine the extent of productivity of the system and contains the code that saves or makes money for the business organization. As a result, business rules should be well-detailed, clean, and comfortable. The codes in the business rule should be the major concern of the developer. The codes should have less plugin making the business rule the most independent component in the system:

Chapter 10

Theme and Purpose Of Software Architecture

This chapter explains the theme and purpose of software architecture. Topics in this chapter include:

- Screaming architecture

- Theme of a software architect

- Purpose of a software architect

- Testable architect

- Clean architect

- Dependency Rule

- Entities and Use case

- Interface Adapter

Screaming Architecture

Let assume we are presented with the document containing the design of a one-family apartment. We will expect to see details such as:

The entrance to the building and a hallway guiding us to the first main room: the living room

Just at a corner behind the living room, we will expect to see the dining area. A set of chairs and a table will likely make this very obvious.

- Close to the dining area is an entrance leading to the kitchen.

- Next to all these details are rooms leading to each of the family room.

No argument, all these details will scream one word: "Home."

Now the question is, what does our software design screams when we are presented with the layout? Does an application entailing the source file in the highest level component and a top-level directory structure scream an accounting software or otherwise? To create a perfect architect, two things are involved. The first is the theme of the software, and the second is the purpose of the software.

The Theme Of The Software Architecture

Just as the architect of a house screamed a house when presented with the design, so should our architect scream its use case. In the design of the house, the use case is the details of the layouts that make the house. Without being told what each room is, we can differentiate a dining room from a kitchen and a kitchen from the living room. Similarly, a system should scream about the use case of its applications.

Frameworks do not determine the software architecture. Hence architecture is not about frameworks. The frameworks of architecture are only tools to be used when designing the theme of the architect. They are not the theme of the architect but used for creating the theme. When an architect is all about the framework, it loses focus from the use case of the architect. A good architect is expected to develop a strategy that prevents the framework from taking over the architecture.

The Purpose of an Architecture

A good architecture revolves around the use case of the system and not the frameworks, environments, or tools of the system. The use case describes the structure of the architecture and, at the same time, explain the purpose of the architect. A good software delays decision about the databases, frameworks, environmental decisions and web server. Framework options are to be left open and not taken as the priority of the architecture. A good architecture delays decision hinging on the Tomcat or Hibernate, Rail or Spring, MySQL and so on. A good architecture emphasis more on the use case and makes it easy to change decisions that do not have any relationship with the use case

Testable Architecture

When your architecture is designed in a way that it focuses on the use case while keeping the frameworks at arm's length, then you will be able to unit-test the framework without affecting the frameworks of the system. To do this, you won't need the webserver or database to run your test. The objects of your entity should be plain, old objects that does not share any form of dependencies on the database or framework or other components. Rather your use case object should control and manage your entity. All of these should be testable in situ.

Clean Architecture

Over the last few decades, we have witnessed different types of ideas on how an architecture system should be designed. These ideas include:

BCE: Introduced by Ivar Jacobson, from his book *Object-oriented Software Engineering: A Use-Case Driven Approach*

HexagonalArchitecture (commonly referred to as Ports and Adapters developed by Alistair Cockburn, was taken on by Steve Freeman and Nat Pryce in their book Growing Object-oriented Software with Tests

DCI from James Coplien and Trygve Reenskaug

All these ideas share a similar objective which is, the separation of concern. These concerns are further divided into a layer. Every layer is made up of at least one layer for business rule and another for the system and user interface. Each of the architecture has similar details and characteristics. These characteristics include:

Testable. The layer containing the business rule can be tested without using the webserver, database, UI, or any other external element.

Framework independence. Frameworks are used as tools because the architecture does not depend on the existence of library or feature-laden software.

Database independent. Since the business rule are not bound to the database, the database could be exchanged with others.

UI independent. This can be easily changed without affecting the use case or changing the remaining elements of the system. A web UI can be exchanged for the console without changing the business rule.

Independent of external agencies. Business rules have nothing to do with the external agencies like the interface

The diagram below shows how a clean architecture should look like. All components are integrated into a single actionable data.

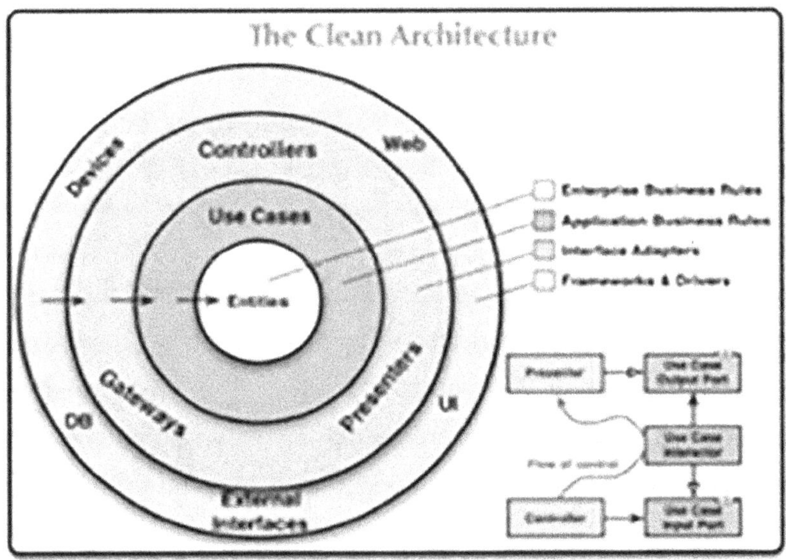

The Dependency Rule

The concentric circles in the above diagram signify the various areas in the software. The further in you go, the higher the software level becomes. The inner circles represent the policies, while the outer is mechanisms. The Dependency is the overall rules that do this software works.

The outermost part of this circle is where the framework, database, and all other external components are located. As a general rule, codes are less written in this area. The only codes that seem to exist here are the glue codes used to communicate to the components in the inner circle.

The components in the inner circle are not expected to know anything about the outer circle. In the same vein, anything declared in the outer circle must not be mentioned by any code in the inner circle. These names include variable, function, classes, and other named software components.

Additionally, when a data format is declared in the outer circle, it should not be disclosed to the inner circles, especially if this format has to do with the framework.

When designing your dependency rule, you may find out that you need more than just four circles to carry out your mission. This is very acceptable as there is no rule binding the number of circles required by a system. However, the dependency rule always comes in. It states that all source code dependencies should go inward. As you do, the level of policy and abstraction increases. It covers a more high-level component until it becomes the most highest and general.

Crossing Boundaries And How To Determine Which Data Cross The Boundary

The lower right hand of the diagram is a perfect example of how data are crossed in a circle. It shows how communications flow between the controller, presenter, and the use case. The flow of control also started with the controller and gradually moved to the use case, before summing it up at the presenter. Also, in the flow of control, each source code point to the use case.

This same method is used to cross all the boundaries in the architectures. To create a boundary that conforms to the rule of dependency, we make use of the dynamic polymorphism to create source code dependency that oppose the flow of control.

From our explanation, we observe that all data that cross the boundary are usually simple data structures. Simple data strut or simple data transfer object can be used depending on the purpose of the architecture. The most important thing to take note of is to ensure that your data structure does not violate any of the data principles.

Entities and Use Case

Entities encompasses the enterprise-wide Critical Business rules and Critical Business Data. Entity could be a set of functions or structure or an object method. Whichever of the two does not matter as much as the entities can be used by different.

The business object is entities that do not have an enterprise but are written on a single application. The object entities encompass the high-level rules. They are the rules that are not affected by any external changes.

As already explained in this chapter, the software comprising of the application-specific business rules is the use case. These rules manage and control the use case in the system, including implementing the use case. The use case controls the flow of data going in and out of the entities and also guide the entities into using the Critical Business rules to achieve the use case goal or objectives.

Change in external elements like the database and interface does not affect the use case. However, change in the operation of the system affects the use case.

Interface Adapter

The interface adapter is a set of adapter in the software layer used to convert data from the most convenient format for the uses case and entities into the format most convenient for the external layers like the interface and the database. The controller, presenters, and viewpoints all belong to the interface adapter layers. The model is more like a database structure that passes from the controller to the use case and then back from the use case to the presenter and views.

In the interface layer, data can be converted from the form most convenient for the use case to the form most convenient for other layers like the database. No code from the interface adapter layer should know anything about the database. If, for example, the database is a SQL, all the SQL should be restricted to this layer or other layers contained in the interface.

Summary

This chapter has extensively explained what screaming architecture is and what makes a clean architecture. The theme and purpose of a software was also explained while paying attention to how boundaries are created and crossed in an architect. Explanation on the interface and the database as an example of low-level components are also given. We also examine the interface adapter. In boundary-crossing, conforming to dependency rules will help prevent errors from occurring and also help create software that is not only testable but also has all the necessary benefits.

Chapter 11

Boundaries

In this chapter, we will cover the following:

- Partial boundaries

- Layers and boundaries

- Test boundaries

Partial Boundaries

Working with a full-fledged architectural design is very expensive and time-consuming. Full-fledged architecture requires that the architect use the input and output data structure, reciprocal polymorphic boundary interface, and all the dependencies that are needed to separate the two sides into independent compilable and deployable components.

As a result of the high cost of human resources and the time needed to run this type of boundaries, architects will design their boundaries in such a way that there is still an avenue to switched to the full-fledged boundaries if need be. This type of boundary design is what is referred to as partial boundaries.

Partial boundaries entail all the necessary independently compilable and deployable components, but these components are kept in a single component as against separating them. What differentiates a partial boundary component from a full-fledged boundary component is that a partial component has all of the details needed for the full-fledged boundaries, but these details are kept in a single component. In a full-fledged boundary, the components are separated and the administration of multiple components is used. In partial boundary, there is no release management burden or version number tracking.

Layers And Boundaries

It is much easier to think of a system as made up of these three components

The database

User Interface

Business Rule

How sufficient these three components depend on the software system the architect is designing. Some system like a computer game might not require more than these three components. Other larger system like a software for a bank loan will require more than these three components.

Test Boundaries

Tests are part of a software system. They also form part of the component of the system and participate in the function of the system. From an architect's point of view, all test is the same irrespective of size or shape. A tiny test like TDD are as complete as a large test like the Cucumber, FitNesse, SpecFlow, and so on.

From the explanation above, it means that the test is complete and well detailed in themselves. By their nature, all test follows the dependency rule; their dependencies are usually inward. Hence, like the database, the test is part of the outermost component of the system circle. Nothing inside the circle depends on the test.

Test are also independently deployable. This is why most times, they are deployed in the test systems and not in the production system. It is the most isolated component of a system; no part of the user case depends on them. Their main function is to support the software development process and not the operation process.

Testability

Developers usually make the mistake of regarding test as outside the system component. This assumption is as a result of the fact that test is not often deployed and are extremely isolated. When a test component is not well integrated into the system, the system becomes too fragile, making it hard to change. This kind of issue arose as a result of the lack of coupling

Test that is well coupled into the system changes along with the system. The simplest change in a system can lead to hundreds of changes in the system. When issues like this occurs, it is known as Fragile Test Problem. A good example of this problem is the group of test that uses the GUI to verify business rule. This type of test will first start in the login structure and navigate to the page structure until they find the particular business rule to be applied to. If this is the case, a slight change in the navigation structure can cause a thousand of a break in the test.

This type of problem can make the system very rigid. This is often a result of the developer avoiding creating any change to avoid the Fragile Test Problem.

The best way to avoid this is to design a testability. The major rule guiding this solution is to avoid dependence on volatile things. The User interface is volatile; any test suite that uses this element will be fragile. Hence it is advisable to create a design and test in which the business rule can be tested without using the GUI.

How To Create Testability

The best way to do this is to create a special API for the test to use and verify the business rules. The API should be very strong and effectively designed in such a way that it can bypass the expensive resources such as the database, avoid security constraint and then force the system into a particular testable states. The API will be a superset of the interactor and interface adapter used by the interface.

The API aim ate decoupling the test from the application. It decouples the structure of the test from the structure of the application.

What Is Structural Decoupling?

This is the strongest form of test decoupling. The API created for the test hides the structure of the application from the test. This action allows the test not to be affected when there is a change in the other components connected with it. The API used to carry out this action should be stored in a separate independently deployable component.

Summary

This chapter covers all that is needed to know about the test. Tests are some separate entities. They are part of the system and needed for the effectiveness and stability of the system. When a test is not designed as part of the system, it makes the system difficult to maintain. Also, the chapter explains the difference between a full-fledged boundary and a partial boundary. It explains the different layers we have in a boundary. In the next chapter, we focus on the details of a system.

Chapter 12

Significant and Non-Significant Architectural Components

The focus of this chapter is on components that are significant to the functions of the software architecture and those that are not. The three software components that will be explicated include presenter, humbling object, and service. Each component will explore based on its contribution to the function or use case of the software architecture. After this explanation, developers will be guided on how to include these components in their system. Below are the outlines that will be covered in this chapter:

- What is a presenter?

- Explanation of the humble object pattern

- Presenter and View

- Great and small service in software architecture

- Importance of service to software architecture

- Avoiding cross-cutting concerns.

What Is A Presenter in Software Architecture?

In software development, a presenter is a form of humble object pattern. It helps the architect in protecting and recognizing architectural boundaries. The question that arises from this definition is, what is the humble object pattern? How is this pattern created and recognized in software development?

What Is An Humble Object Pattern?

The humble object pattern is a design originally created to help developers when testing their units. The pattern makes it easy for developers to separate units that are too difficult to test from those with easy testability. To use this pattern, the developer will divide the units of the system into two parts. The humble module is the unit that contains the hard-to-test elements, while the second part contains all the testable behavior that was stripped out of the humble objects.

A good example of units that are difficult to test is the GUI. This is because it cannot display a written test in the unit on the screen. The developer cannot see if the test written in the GUI is correct or not. But most of the behavior of the GUI is easy to test. Using the humble pattern for the GUI, the developer will separate the GUI behavior that is easy to test from those that are difficult to test. These two parts will be referred to as Presenter and View.

Presenter and View

On the one hand, the humble object unit that contains the elements that are hard to test is referred to as the *View*. The objects in this unit are very simple. The code does not process any data in the GUI; it only moves data to the GUI. On the other hand, the units that contain the testable objects are the *presenter*. The *presenter* receives data from the application, format the data, and then sends it to the *View* who moves it to the screen. Take, for instance, our application wants to display *shopping* data on the screen. A *shopping* object will first be sent to the *presenter*, and the *presenter* will format this object into the required spring and then place it in the *ViewModel,* where the *View* unit can easily locate it. The *View* unit will move the object to the screen.

Each button in the *View model* is given a name by the *Presenter*. This is to make it easy for the View unit to locate the object. If any of the buttons grayed out, the *presenter* will set a *boolean flag* in the *View model.* Since, after formatting the object, the Presenter converts it to converts object string before sending it to the View, what is usually sent by the Presenter to the View mode is either a *string* or a *boolean flag.* After this, all that is required of the View is to send any of these two to the screen. Hence, the View is humble.

The humble pattern is a very good example of Testability. This attribute has long been identified as one of the attributes of good architecture. This is because what defines a software boundary is the separation of units into testable and non-testable parts.

For every good software architecture, at each architectural boundary, the humble object should be found. Since communication at every boundary level usually involves some kind of simple data structure divided into a hard component and an easy one, using a humble pattern at these levels will increase the testable ability of the entire system.

Great and Small Services Of A Software Architecture

Micro-service software and Service-oriented architecture are among the major software architecture we have today. The major reasons for their popularity are:

Services now support the independence of deployment and development

Services are strongly decoupled from each other.

The widespread belief that services, by their nature, are systems is partially true and partially untrue. To start with, software architecture is often defined by their boundaries, and how these boundaries are effectively used to separate high-level policy from low-level details, and also how the boundaries are designed to adhere to the Dependency rule. Services that only separate the behavior of the application are more expensive than services that separate just the function calls. As expensive as they are, they are not necessarily important to software architecture. This type of service is what we will classify as small services.

This is not to say that all the services in a software architecture must be of architectural significance. Services that mainly separate functionality across processes and platforms are also very important, whether they adhere to the rule of Dependency or not.

The main point to note is that services themselves are not very crucial to software architecture.

A simple way to illustrate this is to use the organization of function approach. In the organization of function, the architecture of a monolithic or component-based system is determined by the function calls that adhere to the dependency principle when crossing any architectural boundaries. Other functions that merely separate the behavior of the software from the other are not of architectural significance.

Like function calls, some services are of architectural significant while others are not. In fact, some services are function calls themselves.

Importance of Service to Software Architecture

Decoupling Fallacy

The most noticeable benefit of separating components into service is decoupling. Each service unit is processed independently and can be run even in different processors. This type of service does not have any direct access to each other's variables.

It is important to note that services can only be separated at the level of an individual variable. But, they can still be coupled at the level of resources or at the data level. This statement restrains the decoupling benefit to the level of variables alone.

The Fallacy of Independent Deployment and Development

This benefits hinged on the fact that service can be owned and managed by a dedicated team. This means, the team writes, maintains and operates the service of the software architecture. This kind of independence is assumed to be scalable. This is because a large scale system can be generated and created from hundreds and thousands of services that are independently deployable and developable.

The Problem with this Fallacy

Based on the explanation of the above two fallacies, in building the service of our system, we will want our system to be scalable. To do this, we will build it from different deployable and developable services. After this, we then divide our team of software development into smaller teams, each responsible for maintaining, operating, and writing the service.

Suppose that after creating the service and mapping out areas of concentration to each group in our team, the service is running fine, and each group is owning up to the task given to them. But after a year, a meeting is called, and a new service is to be created. What immediately comes to mind is how many components of the previous service will be altered. The simple fact is everything will have to be changed and recreated.

This problem is inevitable in software architecture. Every software, whether it is service-orient or not, must face this problem. How then do we solve the problem?

Object to The Rescue

How do we solve the problem explained above now that we are using a component-based architecture? Quickly, we go back to our SOLID principle. Part of the principles will prompt us to create a new set of the class whose function can be polymorphically extended to the handle other features. Hence, the feature of the new service will then be incorporated into the new set of the class created. These two components will adhere to the rule of Dependency. The two components are coupled to the abstract based class in the original class using a pattern such as **Template method or Strategy.** Some of the factories under the management of the UI are used to create a class that implements the method.

When the new feature is implemented, the feature of the old service changes, but aside from this change, every other remains a theme. The new system is decoupled and independently deployable and developable.

From the above explanation, it becomes obvious that services do not have to be small monoliths. In fact, a service can be created using the SOLID principle. With this principle, we can add a component class to our system such that part of the component class makes it possible to add more services to our system without altering the components of the former service. With this technique, creating a new system does not necessarily involve redeploying our services. Rather it is a matter of adding new files to our former service. This approach also conform to the Open-Closed Principle

Avoiding Cross-Cutting Concerns

We already started in our previous chapter that architectural boundaries cut through the component that makes our service group and divides them into smaller classes. To handle cross-cutting concerns that state that all significant system services must be designed with an internal component architecture that adheres to the Dependency principle, our services will be designed in such a way that it does not define the architectural boundary of the system. This duty is transferred to the components subsumed within the service.

Summary

In this chapter, we have explored another major aspect of software development. This aspect includes presenter and humble object and the function of service in software development. Every clean architecture will have to conform to the steps guiding the humble object patterning, and the steps guiding the presenter and view and how service is created in software development. While presenter and humble-object patterns are core to the software architecture, services are not of architectural significance

Chapter 13

Clean Embedded Software Architecture

This chapter provides a detail explanation of clean-embedded software; there is more to creating software to just focusing on the working ability. In this chapter, we will be examining the topics highlighted below.

- Clean embedded software architecture

- App-titude test

- Target-hardware bottleneck

- What is the OS?

- Interface programming and substitutability

- Dry conditional compilation derivative

Clean Embedded Software Architecture

In one of the articles by Doug Schmidt, he said something very remarkable, he said:

Although the software does not wear out, firmware, and hardware obsolete, thereby requiring the software modification.

From Doug's statement, it can be inferred that software has a longer life span than firmware or hardware. Hardware, as we know, is continually evolving and improved on. Based on this fact, it is not uncommon for embedded software that is dependent on hardware to be denied a longer life span due to its dependence.

As against popular belief, the firmware does not mean the code is stored inside the ROM. It is not called firmware because of the location where it is stored but because of its dependence and the difficulties encountered when one tries to change it as its hardware evolves.

For non-embedded software developers, the firmware is incorporated into their system whenever SQL is planted in a code or when dependencies are prepared across all the code of the system. Android application developers write firmware when the business login is not separated from the Android API. The best way to avoid creating embedded firmware is to quit writing too many firmware in a program and give your code a chance to live. We will be explaining in detail how embedded software is kept clean to give the software a long life span.

Ap-titude Test

This test shows that the major reason embedded software becomes firmware is that software developers usually focus on getting their codes to work instead of focusing more on the structure of the software in other to increase the life span of the software. Kent Bent summarizes this test in three statements.

- First, make it work
- Then make it right
- Then make it fast

Today, most of the software developers have focused more on the first and third options with little or no attention paid to the second option. The "make it fast" option is usually done by adding micro-optimizations to the program at every interval. Getting the app to work is what is referred to as an *ap-titude test*. There is much more important to software architecture than getting the program to work. When an application is designed with only the working purpose in mind, it is not a clean embedded software architecture.

The Target-Hardware Bottleneck

There are a lot of things developers building embedded software have to take note of that might not be applicable to non-embedded developers. These things include real-time constraints and deadlines, limited space, limited IO, censors and connections, unconventional User Interface, and many more. Usually, the hardware is developed alongside the software. As a software developer, in trying to build codes for this kind of software, difficulties arise. It's the hardware that has its own defect making the software development process slower and time-consuming, or the codes are too difficult to run.

Embedded software and embedded software engineers are indeed very special. But they are not too special to ignore the principles in this book. When embedded software is developed without strict adherence to the principles explained in this book, the *target-hardware bottleneck* problem might arise. The target-hardware bottleneck problem is a situation where codes only run in the target and not around all the components of the software. When this occurs, the system becomes very slow.

Controlling The Target-Hardware Bottleneck

Applying The Layers Control

Layers can come in different ways. In our explanation, we will be using three layers: hardware, firmware, and software. Our hardware will be stationed at the bottom end of the layer. This is in accordance with Doug's rule and Moore's Law. The hardware changes as technology evolve. Part of it will be obsolete, and new ones will come with low cost and more power. To control our system, we fix the hardware at the down part so that whenever changes occur, it will harm the entire system.

To pass the app-titude test, developers often keep the other layers from knowing about the software. This method does not always help the system. In fact, nothing keeps the other layers from knowing about the hardware. Knowledge does not affect the system in any way. If layers are not carefully fixed, the system might become hard to fix, especially when users request a change.

The other two layers comprise the software and the firmware. Be careful of the way you fix the two. When the software and firmware are not well separated and intertwined in a pattern, the code portraying this anti-pattern will resist changes. Changing any component of the system might lead to a disaster. For any small changes, the developer will need to carry out a full regression test

The Hardware

In our program, notice that the line separating the hardware from other layers is more clearly defined than the lines between the software and the firmware. As an embedded developer, one of your major tasks is to firm up the line, cutting across firmware and software. The boundary between these two will create a hardware abstraction layer (HAL). This method has long been in PC way back in the days of Windows.

It is noteworthy that the HAL only exist for the software sitting on its top. Hence the API of the HAL should be integrated with that of the software. For instance, the firmware can be used to keep arrays of bytes and bytes into flash memory. In contract, the application needs to store and read name/value pairs to some persistence mechanism. That the name/value pair is stored in the Flash memory, core memory, spinning disk or cloud should not be the concern of the software, rather the implementation of the flash is a detail that should not be revealed to the software. The HAL provides a service like the flash implementation; it does not reveal to the software how the service is provided. HAL can be used to express the services needed by the application. A Layer can also contain more layers in it, but this should be like a repeating fraction pattern than a set of predefined layers.

In addition to the explanation so far, it is noteworthy that of the qualities of clean embedded software is, it has the ability to be tested off the target-hardware. Therefore, a good and well-defined HAL will provide the necessary substitution point that facilitates off-target testing.

The Processor

It is important to note that whenever an embedded application uses a specialized toolchain, it will need to provide a header file to <1> help you </i>. In C programming language, these compilers often take liberties; new keywords are added to the program to access the processor features. At the end of the application, the program will be similar to a C, but it is no longer a C.

Most times, in other, to give direct access to the processor registers, clock timer, 10 bytes, interrupt controllers, IO port, and other processor functions, the vendor-supplier C compiler provides what looks like global variables. Although it is very helpful to have quick access to these processors function, once these codes are given, the program is no longer a C. It will neither compile with a different compiler for the same processor or for a different processor. Therefore, in other to usc this in a way that it does not create another problem in the future, as the developer, you will have to reduce the files that should know about the C extension.

In some cases, all the software can be designed in such a way that they can be processed independent, but not all the firmware can be. A clean embedded software confines direct access register processors to the firmware. All the application that knows about this register is confined to the firmware and bound to become silicon. In this kind of situation, when you want to make your code work before you build stable hardware, integrating your code together will create some challenges. It will also be challenging to move an embedded application to a new processor.

However, you can use your firmware to isolate low-level functions using some form of processor known as processor abstraction layer (PAL). The firmware above the PAL can be tested off target. This made it a little less firm.

The Operating System

From our explanation of the use of HAL, it can be inferred that in other to create a clean embedded software, the use of HAL is necessary, but this is not sufficient on its own. HAL does not work for all the programs. For instance, using HAL is always enough in bare-metal embedded programs; in this type of program, HAL is used to restrain our codes from getting too close or integrated to the operating system. However, when dealing with an embedded system that uses Real-time operating system(RTOS) or even some embedded version of Window or Linus HAL is inadequate

Therefore, in other to give our embedded software a long lifespan, our operating system should be treated as a detail. Details in software development is a broad topic of its own. This is what the third and last section of this book is all about. The operating system should be used as detail and protected against the OS dependencies. When this is done, the software will be able to access the service of the operating system through the OS.

What Is the Os?

The OS is a boundary layer used to separate the firmware from the software. The OS cannot be directly used; if used directly, it creates a problem. This problem can arise from the situation as inevitable as the RTOS of your program sold to another company making the quality go up or down; the need of the user might even change. Problems will arise from this kind of when your RTOS does not have the requirements for the new needs. To rectify this, you will need to create new technical codes. This type of is not simple synthetic changes because of the direct use of OS. But they will be adapted semantically to the new OS's different capabilities.

Every clean, embedded architecture will separate the software from the operating system. This will be done by using a layer called the operating system abstraction layer (OSAL). Most times, implementing this layer in a program is as easy as trying to change the name of a function; at other times, it will take wrapping several functions together.

Moving software from one RTOL to another is a very difficult task. Instead of the direct use of the OS, you can write a large new OSAL that is very compatible with the old OSAL. The new OSAL layer becomes the place where most of the duplication that comes from using an OS is isolated. This does not need a big overhead. If your

OSAL is already defined, you can encourage your application to have a common structure. To make the valuable application code to be successfully tested off-target and off-OS, the OSAL can be used to provide test points.

Every clean embedded software architecture can be tested off the target operating system. A well-defined OSAL will be capable of providing the seam or set of substitution points that are necessary for off-target testing facilitation.

Interface Programming And Substitutability

When creating a clean-embedded software, aside from the OS and OSAL added to the program, your development process must adhere strictly to all the principles explained in this book. It is with these principles that separation of concerns, interface, and components can be accurately done. The principles will also guild you into achieving valid programming to interface and substitutability.

Programming to interface gives rise to the idea of layered architecture. In this approach, when a module communicates with another module through an interface, service providers can be substituted. One of the most important rules of thumb is to use the header file as interface definitions. When doing this, all care should be taken about what goes into the header. Header file contents should be limited to function declaration, constant and struct names, and so on.

Information like the database structure, typedefs, and the constant that are used by the implementation should not be stored in the interface header. This is not just a matter of clustering the interface header, but this type of cluster can lead to unwanted dependencies. Limit the details of the implementation. The reason for this is simple; details are susceptible to change. Hence the fewer the place where codes know the details, the fewer the places that will have to be modified when implementation change occurs.

Clean embedded software can be tested within the layers because modules always interact through the interface. Each interface provides the substitution points or seams that are off-target testing.

Dry Conditional Compilation Directives

One of the uses of substitutability that is not often taken cognizance of is related to how embedded C++ and C handle different target or operating systems. As a result, the tendency to use conditional compilation to turn segments of codes off or usually occurs. The incessant repetition of codes goes against the principle of DRY (Don't Repeat Yourself). Conditional compilation is used to recognize the types of target-hardware that are often repeated in an embedded system.

Summary

From the explanation of embedded software and the various rules guiding its use and creation, we can say that developers who are interested in creating clean embedded software have a lot to learn. This learning cut across both software architecture and development. Allowing all your codes to become firmware is not good for the lifespan of the software. At the same time, allowing testability only in the target-hardware can impede the lifespan of the software. A clean embedded software encourages off-target testing in all areas of the software.

Chapter 14

Details

In the introduction of this book, it was mentioned that the books are sectioned into three. The first and second has been extensively explained in the thirteen chapters we have explored. The remaining last section will be covered in this chapter and the next. In this chapter, we will cover the following outlines:

- The database is a detail

- The web is a detail

- The framework is a detail

Details are components of the software that are of no architectural significance. This implies that they play no important role in the use case of the software. This type of is located at the outer surface of the program circle already explained. We also stated in our explanation of the circle that elements on the outer part of the circle depend on those on the inner circle. This is in accordance with the Dependency Rule.

The Database is a Detail

Virtually in all the topics so far, we have made mention of this particular element of software architecture. But in this section, this class will be explained in detail.

To start with, the database is a non-entity. This implies that the database is a detail that is not crucial to the architectural level. Often times, programmers and developers the database as the data model. The two concepts are not the same; they represent different things in software architecture. The data model encompasses the structure you give to the data contained inside your application. This feature is very key to the software. Database, however, is a piece of software. It is the item that provides access to the data. In the domain of software architecture, this item is not significant because it is a low-level detail - a mechanism. An excellent architect will not allow this item to stand as an impediment to the neatness or wholeness of the software.

Relational Databases

In the year 1970, Edgar Codd was the first programmer to define the principle of relational database. By 1980, the model grew to become one of the prominent and most widely used forms of data storage. The reason for this prominence is because of the simplicity and usefulness of the principle. It is one of the most important methods of data storage. However, no matter its importance, database remains a low-level detail.

Relational databases use of relational table. In the table, data are arranged in rows. This approach is not only simple but also very neat to use. Notwithstanding, the tables are not known by the use case, and the use case does not need it to perform its action. Hence, the knowledge of this tabular form of utility is only revealed to the low-level functions available outside the circle of our program.

Many developers make the mistake of allowing the database row to go around the system as objects. When this happens, it coupled the business rule, use case and even the User Interface to the relational structure of the data. This creates an architectural error that might be very difficult to correct.

What Makes a Database System so Prevalent?

When we look at software today, it is dominated by database systems like MySQL, Oracle, and so on. Why is this the case? The reason for this is simply the one word: DISK

For more than five decades now, the mainstay of data storage had been the rotating magnetic disk. Most programmers are not even aware of other forms of storage. The size of the disk keeps evolving as technology progresses. It has risen from a huge stack of the massive platter to a thin, simple circle. Its capacity has grown from as low as 20 megabytes to a terabyte or more. However, all throughout its progress, there has been one consistent problem that has to remain indomitable. This problem is that Disk is very slow.

Data are stored in a disk in a circular track. This track is broken into smaller sections of bytes. Each disk platter can have about hundreds of this small track. When you want the read the data in the disk, you have to go to the main track, wait for the disk to rotate to the proper section, read all the 4K of that section into RAM, then index the RAM buffer to get to the track you want. This process is usually time-consuming. It takes milliseconds

When we describe the process it takes to load a track in a disk as time-consuming and describe the time it takes as the millisecond; it feels like this is no time compared to all the other components in the system. However, milliseconds are a lot more than the cycle of time it takes some processors in the system. When data is not stored in a disk, it could be assessed in nanoseconds instead of milliseconds.

To limit the time it takes for the disk to load, you will need a lot of things like indexes, optimized query scheme, caches, and some kind of regular means of representing the data so that the listed items will be able to know what they are working with. You will also need a data access and management system. The system is further divided into two types: file system and relational database management system (RDBMS).

The file system is documented based, while the database system is content-based. The file system provides a very easy way to store documents. When you need to retrieve the name of the document, the file system works very smoothly. However, they are very slow with content and might not even show the content requested.

Database system works very well with the content. They are good at searching out multiple with just the names. However, they don't work well with opaque and vague documents

These two systems make looking for data on disk very easy. Each has its own scheme for indexing and arranging data. When using any of the two, data are quickly brought to its related RAM without much delay.

What Happens when the Disk is No Longer in Vogue?

Today, RAM is gradually taking over, and the need to store data in a disk is gradually dwindling. With this in mind, what happens when disk is no longer available and you have all your data stored in a RAM? How will you organize the data?

The best way to go about this is to organize your data into list trees, queues, or any other data structure and access it using either the pointer or reference. In fact, when you think through the process of storing and retrieving data in a disk, you will notice that even though your data are stored in the database or file system, when you load a file in the RAM, you will have to read and recognize it into any of the data structure of your choice. Data is not read in the tabular rows.

Details

From the above explanation, there is no doubt that the database is indeed a detail. Its main function is to help us move our data back and front the surface of the disk and RAM. The database is no more than a place where we store data.

Therefore, from the architectural point of view, we can say that the data does not play any significant role when it is on the surface of the rotating disk. In fact, during this period, we don't usually acknowledge the presence of the disk.

From our explanation so far, it can be summarized that the organizational structure of the data model is significant to software architecture. However, the system that rotates the data on the surface of the disk is not significant. Therefore, the data is significant, but the database is only a detail and not significant. The relational system works more with the data and not the database.

Web And Framework Details

The Web

Taking a step back into the 1960s in the wake of the webserver. When we try to compare the web in those days to what we have today, we will see a big difference that will confirm to us that the web has indeed changed. But how true is this assumption? Did the web really change?

The web is a series of oscillation that moves back and forth between putting all the computer power inside a central server or putting all the computer power out at the terminal. This oscillation did not start with the web. Before the advent of the web, this kind of oscillation exists in the client-server architecture, central minicomputer, and so on.

Now a good look at the overall scope of the history of IT, we will come to one realization. The web didn't change anything at all. The oscillation of the web is central that should be separated from our business rules.

This upshot is very simple since the GUI is a detail, the web is a GUI, and it is a detail. As a web developer, details such as the web, database, and GUI should be separated from boundaries away from the functional components of the system.

A Framework is a Detail

This is another interesting component in a software system. The first important thing to note about the framework is that the framework is not architectures. Frameworks authors are not software developers. Framework authors write frameworks to solve a particular problem. For instance, when you buy a framework, you read through it to know how to use it in your software. In the documentation, the framework author explains how to incorporate the framework with your system and urge you to couple the framework with your system.

From the point of view of the framework author, coupling the framework with your system is not a risk because he has control over the system. Obeying this instruction can result in any of the following risks:

Frameworks do not usually follow the Dependency rule hence their architecture is not always clean

At the early stage of your application, the framework might be very helpful, but this stops as soon as your application progress

You may get stuck once the framework evolves in a direction you are not interested in

You may wish to switch to a better framework but find this almost impossible

Solutions

The best solution to this not to couple your program with the framework. Once you get the framework to work, treat it as a detail and not part of the inner cycle of the architecture. Let it remain on the outer surface.

Do not allow the framework into your vital codes. Instead of doing this, follow the dependency rule and integrate it into one of the plugins for your vital codes

Although, there are frameworks that require that you couple your program with it. For instance, when you are using C++, you will have to merge STL with your program. If it's Java, you will couple the standard library. This is expected and normal. However, it is important to note that when you merge a framework with your application, you are stuck with the framework for the period you will use that application.

Summary

From our explanation so far, it becomes obvious that details are not as crucial to the software architecture as we used to think

Chapter 15

Implementation and Case Study

All the aspect we have treated in the fourteen chapters of this book, if followed accordingly, it will help us to create a superb software designed with excellent boundaries, clearly defined responsibilities, and well-managed dependencies. The principles explicated in this book are guidelines for building very clean software. However, there are some things to take note of in the implementation of the software. If this is not well followed, it might make all our efforts come to waste.

To start with, let's assume we want to build an application for an online book store. Among the requirements of the application is that the customers can see the list of their orders. This kind of application seems like something we can do on Java programming language alone, but it can actually be done with another programming. The first step to designing this application is to organize our codes and design. Below are the steps to organize our application into layers. The method explained below is for the four different patterns we can use to separate our layers.

Package by Layer

This type of layer is achieved by using the traditional horizontal layered architecture. Here are codes are separated based on the functions they perform in the system. This system of separation is called package by layer.

For our application, we have three layers in all. Our three layers are split into a layer for business logic, a layer for code, and a layer for persistence. What we have done here is to split our codes into layered grouped according to the function they perform in the application.

Package by Feature

This type of separation or packaging can also be adopted for our codes. In this approach, implementation is separated based on their classes using vertical boundaries for related features. The class is then placed in a single Java package. The package is given a name to reflect the concepts in it. The top side organization of this type of code reflects something about the business domain. Thus, the code class has more to do with a domain other than with repositories or web. As a result, it is very easy to find all the codes that need modifying when need be. This is because they are all in a single Java package and not distributed around the program. Because of the simplicity of this type of separation, programmers often find it difficult to use horizontal layering and switch to vertical layering.

Ports And Adapters

Approaches like the hexagonal architecture, ports and adapters, controllers, boundaries, and entities all aim to create an architecture where the business domain is separated from details like the database, framework, and GUI. This type of separation is in relation to the circle explained in previous chapters of this book. Outside the circle, we have classes like the UI, database, and framework, while all the domain concepts are stored inside the circle. The rule guiding this type of separation is, the outside depends on the inside and not the other way round. In our circle, we will separate the two classes as domain and infrastructure. This is shown in the diagram below:

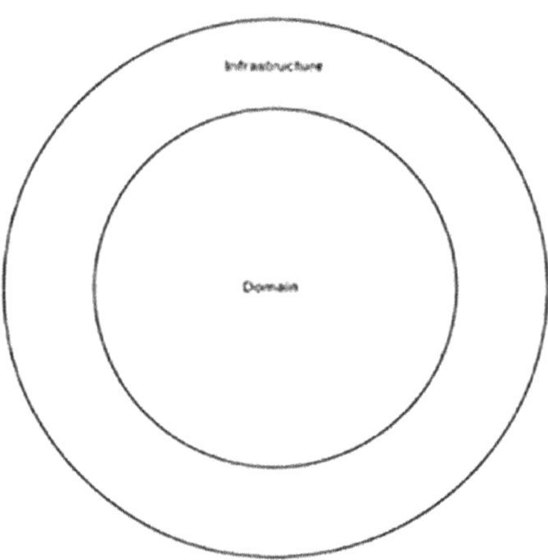

Package By Component

Now let's assume that in our program, we used the layered package. This means, all the dependencies downward while the next layer depends on the next adjacent layer. This will help us achieve a clean acyclic dependencies graph. However, the problem with using this layer is that we can cheat by adding some dependencies, and our graph will still meet the acyclic dependencies.

Let's assume that someone new was hired to join the team. Now the new person was given an **order**-related list to implement. The newcomer will want to impress the team by making the use of case work as timely as he can. When the newcomer starts his work, he noticed a class called **ordercontrol** and guessed that must be the place the code he needs for the implementation is stored. The newcomer also noticed another class and injected his implementation into the other controller class. After his work, the webpage is working, but the UML is faulty.

The dependency arrow is still downward, but some changes have been created in the program. This type of program is known as a relaxed layer architecture.

The best way to avoid this kind of situation is a guideline. This should be in the form of an architectural principle that says, web controller should never access repositories directly. What is left with this rule is enforcement.

The above situation brings us to package by component. This is simply a hybrid approach to what we have been treating so far. The goal of this bundling is to place all responsibilities related to a single coarse-grained component into a single Java package. Package by components keeps the users interface separately the same way ports and adapter treat the web as just a delivery mechanism. This approach integrates the business logic and persistence code into a single component. Uncle Bobs defines a component as a unit of deployment. They are the smallest part of a system that can be deployed as an entity. Component in Java programming is known as jar files. In this book, we will define a component as a related functionality grouped behind a neatly designed interface residing inside an architectural environment like the application.

Among the importance of package by component is, when writing a code that has to do with order. You can easily go to the category of *ordercomponent*. This will direct you to a component where there is a separation of concern. This means that the business logic will be separate from the business data.

*Proble*m with The Implementation Details

On the surface, these four separation techniques, all like different approaches that can be used for different types of applications. However, when any of these packages is wrongly used, it will affect the software. A very popular modifier that programmers have adopted without a thought about its effect on the program is the public access modifiers. This modifier seems ingrained in the muscle memory of programmers. This type of modifier is very common in codes sample for tutorial, books and open-source framework on GitHub. This modifier is popularly used, irrespective of the package adopted in the program, whether horizontal or vertical, port or adapter.

The disadvantage of this is, by making all your program public, you are not taking very good advantage of all the encapsulation facilities made available by your programming language. This brings us to the question, organization, or encapsulation, which is better?

When you make all your program public, it means one thing, the packages are organizational and cannot be used for encapsulation. By organization, it means the program is groupings like a folder. Therefore, the use of packages can be ignored since public program can be used from anywhere in the code. Using a package in such a program does not provide any real value. When the packages are ignored, because they don't really provide any encapsulation assistance, the program you are creating might not be problem-free.

When all your Java type program is made public, what we have in such type of program are four ways to describe a horizontal program. But in doing this, the programmer has to be very careful. The access modifier in the Java program is not very neat. The fewer the public type we have in a program, the smaller its dependencies potential.

If the program you are building is a monolithic program, where all the codes reside in a single source code tree, it is advisable to lean on your compiler to enforce your architectural principle, instead of relying on self-discipline and post-compilation tooling.

From the explanation so far, it is advisable that when building a program, pay attention to the implementation. If this is not done correctly, it could destroy the program in a flash. Ensure you pay attention to how to map your desired design on the code structure, how the code will be organized, and which decoupling method to apply. Leave an option where it is needed and take consideration of the size of your team and their level of skill.

Case Study

Here we are going to be applying all we have learned so far in this book. The program we will be using is software for selling videos. The basic information about the program is that we have a couple of videos we want to sell, and we want to sell these to both individuals and businesses on the web. The price range between streaming the application and downloading it will be stated in the application. An individual can act as both the viewer and the purchaser.

The first step towards creating our program is to identify the architecture of the system. Hence we recognized the use case and the actors.

Use Case

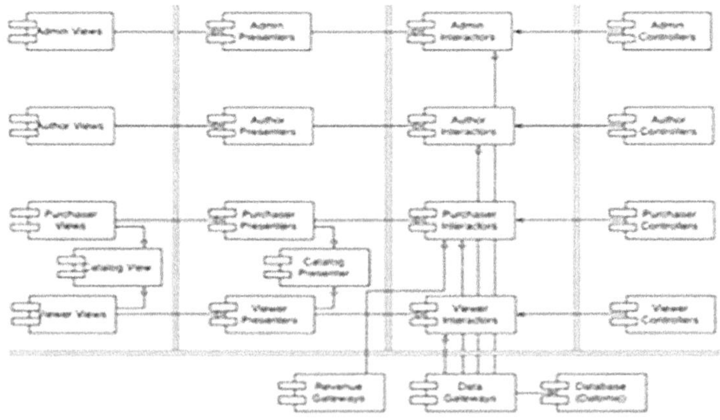

The diagram above is a good example of a well-detailed use case. Here we have four actors, each with its own use case. And according to the Single Responsibility Principle, these actors will be responsible for any changes in our program. Whenever a change or a new feature is required, the change will be directed to the actor that needs it. Hence our next step is to separate our actors so that change in one actor's program does not create changes in another.

Observe the dash in the use case. These are abstract use cases. This is the type of use case used to set a general principle for another use case to figure out. In our program, this is obvious in the relationship between the three-view catalog. The *View Catalog as Viewer* and *View Catalog as the Purchaser* use case both inherit from the *View Catalog* use case.

Although the abstraction is not very necessary, it was used because the two use case is very similar.

Component Architecture

Now that we have settled the part of the use case and the actors, we will look into the component architecture.

The drawing lines in the program represent the architectural boundaries. Each of our components has been broken down into their various actors. The controller, view, presenter, and interactor has been partitioned into components. Each of these components also represents a jar file. Each component has its own view, controller, presenter, and interactor.

The abstract use case is dealt with in a very special way. The special component for the Catalog View and the Catalogue Presenter are made like this so that inheriting components will contain both the presenter a and view that will inherit for those abstract components.

The method of partitioning adopted in the program will also make it easy to combine our independent deliverables into five jar file. One is for the presenter, one for view, one for the controller, one for interactor, and the last one for utilities. With this, components that are likely to change for the same reason and at different times will be independently separated.

Managing Dependencies

In our program, control is managed from the left-hand side to the right-hand side. This means that input occurs at the controller and processed in the interactor. After this, the presenter format the result before the Views display it.

While our control flows from right to left, we saw that the arrows do not follow this order. Rather most of the arrows point from left to right. This is so because we are building our program to follow the Dependency rule. Therefore, all dependencies in our program crossed the boundary line in one direction and points to the component containing the higher-level policy.

Two arrows are worth exploring: the *using* arrow and the *inheritance* relationship. The *using* arrow(open arrows) point to the flow of control while the *inheritance* arrow (closed arrows) point against the flow of control. These two depict our Open-Closed Principle. We used this principle to ensure that dependencies flow in the right direction. With this, any change in the low-level does not affect the high-level.

Summary

We will observe that in our program, we made use of two dimensions of separation. The first is the Dependency Rule, and the second is the Single Responsibility Principle. These two are used to separate component that changes for different reasons from the components that change at a different rate. Different reasons applied to the actor while different rates applied to the different levels of policy. With this, the program can be deployed the way it suits us. Components can be grouped into deployable in any way we want and this can be changed without affecting the system itself

Conclusion

Building a clean software architecture should be the goal of all developers who aim to stand out among the numerous we have today. In each chapter of this book, we have covered a lot of principles and guidelines for creating impeccable software. Principles ranging from how to group elements into class, how these elements are applied to the software architecture, and the roles of each were extensively explained.

Also, principles guiding software components and how the components are compiled and deployed were elucidated. We also explained how interaction is facilitated and controlled between components.

In our explanation, we pointed out reasons why elements such as the database, GUI, and frameworks are not of architectural significance to the software. These elements are mere mechanisms used in carrying out one function or the other. As a result, software developers are advised not to allow these elements into the inner circle of their system. The inner circle is the domain of the system. This is where components such as the business rule, policy, use case, entities and other elements of architectural significance are managed. The elements outside the circle are to depend on the elements inside the circle. This is the main point in the Dependency rule.

Software developers are advised to adhere strictly to all the rules explained in this book. The SOLID Principles are as important as the principles guiding component coupling and cohesion. None should be left out. Software developers are also advised to be thorough with the implementation process. This is because failure to look critically at this might lead to the ruin of the software.

The best way to start creating software is to start with the structure. The structure encompasses the system itself. It helps in managing how each element of the system will be fixed into the component of the system. The structure is more critical to the system than the behavior. A good structure will make the system susceptible to change. Starting with the behavior might make the software too rigid to change.

All clean software is testable at each level of the system. Testability is very crucial. Now it's time for you to get started writing clean code!